4.75 West. h. 37%

YOU CAN LEARN RUSSIAN

You Can Learn
RUSSIAN

by Marguerita Rudolph

Illustrated by John Kaufmann

BOSTON   TORONTO
LITTLE, BROWN AND COMPANY

Published simultaneously in Canada
by Little, Brown & Company (Canada) Limited

PRINTED IN THE UNITED STATES OF AMERICA

To my daughter Alicia
whose influence continues to be important in all my work

· ✠ ✳ ✠ ✳ ✠ ·

Introduction

Is Russian a very difficult language?

Not really — when you are interested in learning it.

One day a few years ago practically everybody in the world learned a purely Russian word overnight! That word, as you might have guessed, is "spoot-nik" (*spoo* — as in *spool of thread*). In Russian the word "spootnik" is not only an astronomical word meaning *satellite*, but also a common, friendly word meaning somebody going along, someone journeying with you.

Is Russian difficult?

Not entirely. Being an advanced language, like English, it has a large technical vocabulary that is very much like the English one. When you start learning Russian you will immediately recognize many words. (Sometimes the stress may be on a different syllable. We show the stress in SMALL CAPITALS.)

For example, the Russian words "AH-drehs," "av-to-mo-BEEL," "MOO-zi-ka," "in-stroo-MENT," "lee-tyeh-rah-TOO-ra," do not seem strange. "Moo-zi-ka" is spelled with a *k* in Russian because in Russian every word with a *k* sound is spelled with a *k*. In fact practically all Russian words are written the way they sound. Just think how difficult English is in this respect: you learn to spell *key* with a *k*, but *cat* with a *c*; and then you have to remember that the word *knee* for some reason has a *k* that you never hear.

In Russian, most words are as easy to spell as "Mama" — that's a Russian word, printed in Russian letters. There is not even any word in common usage that means *spelling* in Russian; there is only the word for *writing!* This means if you can write you can spell — in Russian.

True, then, that Russian is *not* difficult when it comes to spelling and learning technical and scientific words. But what about reading, and grammar, and pronunciation? Aren't those difficult?

Yes, they are. Russian has a different alphabet, which you will gradually master as you read this book. Russian also has grammatical complexities, with many rules, and of course many exceptions to those rules. Yet *some* of its grammar is easier than English. For example, in English you would say, *"The* tea *is* on *the* table." In Russian you would simplify that sentence to "Tea on table." And that would be correct.

Russian is also difficult to learn because it is such a rich language, with many ancient and native words and with words that keep changing to form diminutives and soft endearments. For example, "babushka" and "dyeh-dooshka" — the regular words used for *grandmother* and *grandfather* — really mean *dear little grandmother* and *dear little grandfather*. Even the word "vodka" is a diminutive of "voda" (*water*); it literally means *little water*, if you analyze it, but in everyday usage it means the native Russian alcoholic drink.

Besides being so full of diminutives, the Russian language has many words and expressions which are interesting to compare with English ones. For instance, the Russian word for *handkerchief* — "nosovoy platochek" — really means *little kerchief, for the nose*. And the Russian word for *Thank you* is a slow, soft word: "Spahseebo." It is derived from the word for *God bless you*.

In the nine chapters of this book you will get acquainted with many hundreds of words, and you may not think it so difficult to learn Russian when you realize that millions of people do learn it (including two-year-old Russian babies).

Schoolchildren in many parts of the world are learning Russian, and more and more Americans every year are interested in Russian and able to learn it (including some older people). My aim, therefore, is to challenge and encourage you to do the same.

So let's learn Russian — now.

MARGUERITA RUDOLPH

Contents

YOU CAN LEARN RUSSIAN

Chapter 1

The Russian Alphabet —
in Sight and Sound

Russian is quite an old language: it is more than eight centuries old. And, like any language, it has been changing with the times. New words, relating to new events and new inventions, have been added to the language; and old words no longer useful have been left behind. Other changes in the language have helped to do away with unnecessary rules, and some unnecessary letters as well. So it is easier to learn Russian now than it would have been forty-five years ago.

The Russian alphabet now consists of thirty-three letters. Here they are, capital and small, in Russian alphabetical order.

А	а	К	к	Х	х
Б	б	Л	л	Ц	ц
В	в	М	м	Ч	ч
Г	г	Н	н	Ш	ш
Д	д	О	о	Щ	щ
Е	е	П	п	Ъ	ъ
Ё	ё	Р	р	Ы	ы
Ж	ж	С	с	Ь	ь
З	з	Т	т	Э	э
И	и	У	у	Ю	ю
Й	й	Ф	ф	Я	я

Some of these letters must look familiar. Some may seem partly recognizable; some are strange. You may be glad you know another language and another alphabet with which to compare the Russian. And — maybe Russian will increase your knowledge of English.

Let's compare the Russian alphabet with the English, by placing the two side by side.

Russian		English		Russian		English	
А	а	A	a			Q	q
Б	б	B	b	Р	р	R	r
		C	c	С	с	S	s
В	в			Т	т	T	t
Г	г			У	у	U	u
Д	д	D	d			V	v
Е	е	E	e	Ф	ф		
Ё	ё			Х	х		
		F	f			W	w
Ж	ж			Ц	ц		
		G	g			X	x
		H	н	Ч	ч		
З	з			Ш	ш		
И	и	I	i	Щ	щ		
Й	й			Ъ	ъ		
		J	j	Ы	ы		
К	к	K	k	Ь	ь		
Л	л	L	l	Э	э		
М	м	M	m	Ю	ю		
Н	н	N	n	Я	я	Y	y
О	о	O	o			Z	z
П	п	P	p				

First we look carefully at the Russian on the left, then at the English on the right.

No doubt it seems easy and pleasant to come back to the familiar English letters after looking hard at Russian ones!

How do the alphabets compare — the Russian and the English? As you see, the Russian alphabet has thirty-three letters, and the English twenty-six. However, two of the Russian letters are not properly letters in themselves, and are actually called *signs*, not letters: ъ = *hard sign* and ь = *soft sign;* they give special sounds to the letters next to them, explained later on (Chapter 8). You learn these best by hearing them.

When you look more carefully at the Russian alphabet you will notice that all but three letters have the same design whether they are capital or small.

The only letters with different designs are:

А а   Б б   Е е

In the English alphabet, most of the letters — seventeen of the twenty-six — have different designs for capital and small letters.

Written Russian letters, or "script," like the English, have different designs from the printed ones. (You may see them at the end of this chapter.)

In the Russian alphabet there are twenty consonants:

Б В Г Д Ж З К Л М Н П Р С Т Ф Х Ц Ч Ш Щ

In the English alphabet — also twenty:

B C D F G H J K L M N P Q R S T V W X Z

Let's examine the consonants closer. Fourteen Russian consonants have English letters that correspond, not always in looks or order, but in *sounds*. Which are they? Let the Russian and English equivalents face each other, so you can get better acquainted with them:

Russian Consonants	*English Consonants*
Б	B
В	V
Г	G
Д	D
З	Z
К	K
Л	L
М	M
Н	N
П	P
Р	R
С	S
Т	T
Ф	F

We can see that some of these fourteen Russian and English consonants have a good deal in common besides the most important feature — sound. For example, the Russian Б is like the English B without the upper right-hand curve; both have the same alphabetical order. The K, M and T are identical. The Russian B, H, C and P certainly have familiar designs — though different sounds from the same designs in English.

This leaves only six consonants that look quite different from the English — the Russian G, D, Z, L, P, F. Look at them:

Г Д З Л П Ф
G D Z L P F

What is more important to us now than the looks is the *sounds* made by pronouncing the letters. Since fourteen of the twenty Russian consonants are similar to the English, Americans can learn to say most Russian words quite easily. For instance, when the Russian name "Gagarin" (the first astronaut) became known to us, English-speaking people learned it easily because they have hard *g* and *r* and *n* sounds in their language. The same applies to the word "spootnik": the s-p-t-n-k consonants are the same in the English language, even though *s*, *p* and *n* in Rus-

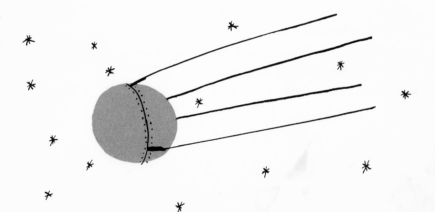

sian *look* different. And because both languages have fourteen consonants in common, you can easily learn to say such words as "lunik," "troika," "soviet," "samovar" and "vodka" the way a native Russian says them. For the same reason, Russians can say American names like *Kennedy* and *Roosevelt* and pronounce recognizably the consonants in English words like *baseball* and *football*.

However, six of the twenty Russian consonants have *no* corresponding English ones. Here they are:

Ж Х Ц Ч Ш Щ

And here are those consonants in Russian words (in parenthesis we give the nearest possible English sounds, and, in words of more than one syllable, the syllable that is stressed is in CAPITAL LETTERS):

жить (zheet) (pronounce *zh* as *s* in pleasure) — *to live*
ха-ха-ха (kha-kha-kha) — printed for the sound of
    laughter — "*ha-ha.*"
центр (tsehntr) — *center*
чай (chay; pronounced to rhyme with *shy*) — *tea*
школа (SHKAW-la) — *school*
щека (shcheh-KAH) — *cheek*

Thus ц comes close in sound to either *ts* as in *lots* or the second *c* in *concert;* ч is *ch,* ш is *sh,* and щ is *shch.*

Since there are twenty consonants both in Russian and in English, and fourteen have corresponding sounds, there are also of course six English consonants that have *no* corresponding Russian ones. These peculiar *English* consonants are C, H, J, Q, W, X. For that reason, many English names are difficult to say and even more difficult to write in Russian. For example, *Washington* comes out "Vahshington," and *Mark Twain*, "Mark Tven," because there is no letter *w* in Russian. And since there is no *h*, there is no *th* sound, and the word *Smith* comes out "Smeet" — almost unrecognizable. Still, many words which the Russian and the English languages use in common are easily recognizable. The Russian words "geografia," "matematika," "astronavt" or "kosmonavt," for example, can be recognized by Americans, while the English words *geography*, *mathematics*, *astronaut* can be recognized by Russians.

Russian vowels are less similar to the English than the consonants. There are eleven vowels in Russian:

А   Е   Ё   И   Й   О   У   Ы   Э   Ю   Я

There are six vowels in English:

A   E   I   O   U   and sometimes   Y

Some of the Russian vowels have corresponding vowels or sounds in English:

Russian	*English*
А	*ah* as in *father* (stressed), or as in *comma* (at end of word, or when not stressed)
Е	*eh* as in *red* or *yeh* as in *yellow*
Ё	*yo* or *yaw*
И	*ee* as in *beet*
О	usually *o* as in *obey;* also (stressed) as *aw* in *bore;* sometimes as in *love* or as in *pot.* (We have *o* differences in English!)
У	*oo* as in *poor* or *look*
Ю	*yu* (something like *u* in *humor*)

The Russian vowel A — called "Ah" — like the English *a*, is the first letter of the alphabet. You may wish to compare the alphabetical order numbers of the other letters.

VOWELS

Russian	Alphabetical Order	English	Alphabetical Order
А	1	A	1
Е	6	E	5
Ё	7	I	9
И	10	O	15
Й	11	U	21
О	16	Y	25
У	21		
Ы	29		
Э	31		
Ю	32		
Я	33		

CONSONANTS

Russian	Alphabetical Order	English	Alphabetical Order
Б	2	B	2
В	3	V	22
Г	4	G	7
Д	5	D	4
З	9	Z	26
К	12	K	11
Л	13	L	12
М	14	M	13
Н	15	N	14
П	17	P	16
Р	18	R	18
С	19	S	19
Т	20	T	20
Ф	22	F	6

When you look at the alphabetical order of the consonants, you can see that B, R, S and T have identical
alphabetical numbers; and six letters come close to having
the same order.   Which are they?

We know now that some of the thirty-one sounded
letters and the two signs of the Russian alphabet look different from the English, yet, like the English, are made
up of lines and curves of different sizes and directions.

When you look at books printed in Russian you can
recognize something else that is entirely familiar.   Look
at this paragraph from a children's story, *Little Chick*.[1]

Цыплёнок остался у забора один.   Вдруг он видит:
взлетел на забор красивый большой петух, вытянул
шею вот так и во всё горло закричал: "Кукареку!" и
важно посмотрел по сторонам: "Я ли не удалец? Я
ли не молодец?"

You must have noticed the dots and curlicues of punc-
tuation:

   .   — the period
   ,   — the comma
   ?   — the question mark, at the end of a question
  " " — quotation marks, at both ends of the quotation

[1] K. Chukovsky: *Little Chick* (Government Publishers of Children's
Books, Moscow, USSR, 1955).

The Russians use the same little symbols in construction and control of written sentences and phrases as are used in English.

You may also have noticed that, like English, there are no accents above any Russian letters. But, in giving the pronunciation, we have put SMALL CAPITALS to show how a syllable is stressed; the stress is very important in Russian words, as in English. For instance, "Oka" (Oh-KAH).

In the following page from a Russian calendar you can see that the Russian numbers are the same as English when printed.

СЕНТЯБРЬ

Понедельник		7	14	21	28
Вторник	1	8	15	22	29
Среда	2	9	16	23	30
Четверг	3	10	17	24	
Пятница	4	11	18	25	
Суббота	5	12	19	26	
Воскресенье	6	13	20	27	

You can also see that the month is divided into seven-day weeks; but the first day of the week, by the calendar, is Monday and the last is Sunday. Holidays are usually printed in red letters, just as they often are on American calendars. But notice that days of the week are printed down the columns of the Russian calendar instead of across it, as is usual in America.

In the Russian language, as in the English, certain important government names appear familiarly only in their initials. Here are three of them:

C C C P   The letters are SSSR. They stand for "Sayuz Savyehtskeekh Sotseeah-leesteechehskeekh Rehspoobleek," which means Union of Soviet Socialist Republics — USSR in English.

C Ш A   The letters are SSHA. They stand for "Soyehdeenyonnieh Shtati Ahmehreekee," meaning the United States of America — USA.

O O H   The letters are OON, standing for "Orgahneezahtseeyah Obyehdee-nyonnikh Nahtseey," which means the United Nations Organization — UN.

HERE IS RUSSIAN SCRIPT OR
WRITTEN LETTERS

(to compare with the printed ones)

А	а	*A*	*a*		Р	р	*P*	*p*
Б	б	*Б*	*б*		С	с	*C*	*c*
В	в	*B*	*в*		Т	т	*T*	*m*
Г	г	*Г*	*г*		У	у	*У*	*у*
Д	д	*Д*	*g*		Ф	ф	*Ф*	*ф*
Е	е	*Е*	*е*		Х	х	*X*	*x*
Ё	ё	*Ё*	*ё*		Ц	ц	*Ц*	*ц*
Ж	ж	*Ж*	*ж*		Ч	ч	*Ч*	*ч*
З	з	*З*	*з*		Ш	ш	*Ш*	*ш*
И	и	*И*	*и*		Щ	щ	*Щ*	*щ*
Й	й	*Й*	*й*		Ъ	ъ	—	*ъ*
К	к	*К*	*к*		Ы	ы	*ы*	*ы*
Л	л	*Л*	*л*		Ь	ь	—	*ь*
М	м	*М*	*м*		Э	э	*Э*	*э*
Н	н	*Н*	*н*		Ю	ю	*Ю*	*ю*
О	о	*О*	*о*		Я	я	*Я*	*я*
П	п	*П*	*п*					

HERE ARE SOME RUSSIAN
WORDS IN SCRIPT

Америка   Азия   Африка   Европа

Атлантический   океан

In English, much the same in sound:

America   Asia   Africa   Europe

Atlantic Ocean

Chapter 2

Five Russian Letters
Just like English [1]

А а К к М м О о Т т

You have already started learning and recognizing Russian words, and now you will start reading Russian. But first you must learn to read all the letters in the alphabet — a few in each chapter. We'll begin with the easiest ones.

Although the Russian alphabet is different from the English, it does have five letters that are the same. They are:

[1] Except for one slight difference: in Russian, capital and small м and т have the same design; in English, the small *m* and *t* are different from their capitalized form.

A — called "Ah" — pronounced *ah* as in *father;* or (usually at the end of a syllable) a shorter *a*, as in *comma*.

К — called "Kah" — pronounced *k* as in *key;* it is never silent.

М — called "Emm" — pronounced just like the English *m*.

О — called "Aw" — usually pronounced as in *obey;* sometimes more stressed, *aw*, as in *bore*. It also has a sound *ah*, like the English *o* in *pot;* and it may be like *uh* as in *love* — it behaves differently in the company of different letters, as does the English *o*. You learn by hearing.

Т — called "Teh" — is pronounced either "soft," as with the English *t* in *unity* or *kitty;* or hard, as in *not* and *cat*.

These five letters appear very frequently. Let's open a Russian book to see them. The book is called "Шутки" (SHOOT-kee), meaning *Jokes*.[1] Here is a two-line, nine-word children's verse:

Original Russian	*English Translation*
ГОСТИ	*GUESTS*
Как приятно чай попить,	How pleasant to have tea, and chat
О том, о сём поговорить!	About this, and that!

[1] E. Charushin: *Jokes* (Government Publishers of Children's Books, Moscow, USSR, 1946).

Look at the letters in the Russian verse. In it A appears twice, К appears twice, M also twice; O is there nine times, T five times; and T and К appear in the Russian title of the book.

Now look at the Russian verse again. You can read some of the words:

> как (kahk) — *how;* a common word (used, for instance, as the first word in the Russian for *How are you?*)
>
> о (aw) — *about,* a preposition
>
> о том (aw tome; rhymes with *Rome*) — *about that*

O, like the English O, can also be an exclamation. "О мама!" is read just as if it were English, and you can also say "Ah-Ah-AH" when you open your mouth to oblige the doctor, with the same expression and meaning in Russian as in English.

You are now starting to build a Russian vocabulary with five letters.

There is another Russian word you can read, one which needs no translation since it is the same word in English:

> атом (ah-tawm)

How many simple Russian words can we learn with these five letters A, К, M, O, T?

We'll count, and include those you've already learned. (This may remind you of playing a game of anagrams!)

We can now also learn two geographic words:

Ока (Oh-кан) — the Oka, a Russian river, tributary
　　of the Volga

Кама (Кан-ma) — also a Russian river, the Kama,
　　flowing into the Volga

Since language is not made up of separate words standing still, we need to learn to use these Russian words in
sentences in order to learn Russian.

"Кто там?" is a correct way to ask, in Russian, *Who
　　is there?* "Is" is not required in Russian.

The correct Russian answer, then, is:

"Там кот" — *There [is] [the] cat;* or, in better Eng-
　　lish, "*The cat is there.*"

As you see, there are no articles in Russian: you don't
say *a* cat or *the* cat, but simply *cat,* "кот."

One can also answer "Кто там?" with:

"Кот там." (With emphasis on "там" it would mean:
　　"*The cat is* THERE.")

"Там? О, тот кот!"

We will have more opportunity to use these words in
sentences in later chapters; meanwhile, look over the
Russian words you already know and find a rhyme for:

　　　　　от　　　　　　　　то　　　　　　　как

Now find the rivers Ока and Кама on the map of the
CCCP.

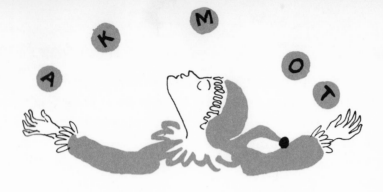

1 акт (ahkt) — *act*, as an *act* in a play
2 атом (AH-tawm) — *atom*
3 как? (kahk) — *how?*
4 какао (kah-KAH-o) — *cocoa*
5 кот (kawt) — *cat*
6 кто? (ktaw) — *who?*
7 мак (mahk) — *poppy;* flower or seed
8 мама (MAH-ma) — *mama*
9 о (aw) — *about,* or *oh, O;* о том (aw tome) *about that*
10 от (awt) — *from* (a preposition)
11 так (tahk) — *thus.* Or, *this way.* (An answer to "как?")
12 там (tahm, like the name Tom) — *there*
13 то (taw) — *that,* as *that child*
14 ток (tawk) — *current,* as *electric current*
15 тот (tawt) — *that,* as *that man* (or any masculine noun)

So — we have learned fifteen words. And if we count o as two words (*about* and *oh*) and "том," we have seventeen words that we can read with the five letters A K M O T.

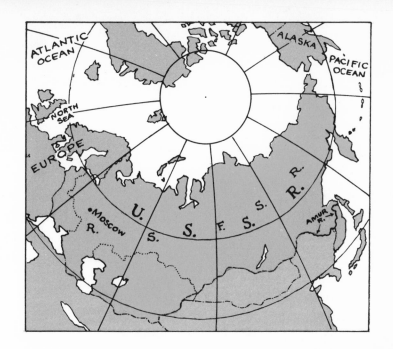

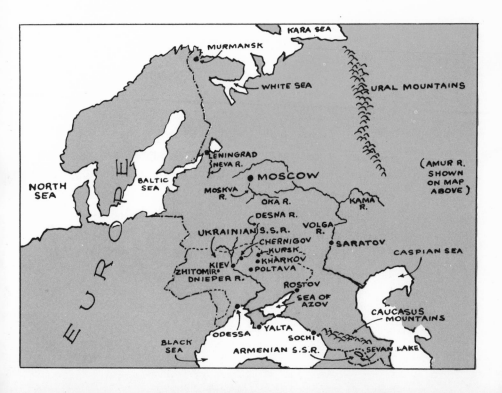

Chapter 3

Three Russian Letters Similar to English

E e　　З з　　С с

The Russian letters you already know — A, К, M, O, T — are the same as English ones. The three letters you will learn in this chapter only look similar to others in English. Be careful not to confuse these Russian letters with the English!

　　E — called "Ye" — is pronounced "yeh" (as *yellow*) at the beginning of a word or when it follows a vowel; it is pronounced "eh" (as in *red*) after certain consonants and after others has a soft sound you will learn by hearing Russian spoken. (We translate it as *yeh*, because you say it almost that way.) E looks like the English *e*, but it does not always sound like it.

　　З — called "Zeh" — is pronounced the same as the English *z* (in *zebra*). The Russian З — Zeh — and the English *z* look the same in script: *з* — but in print, as you see, з looks like the numeral 3.

С — called "Ess" — is always pronounced *s* (as the English *c* in *center*).

You now know eight Russian letters. Here they are in alphabetical order:

А Е З К М О С Т

Let's see those letters in printed words in a Russian book.

Here are a few lines of dialogue from a fairy tale well known to Russian and American children, retold by the famous Russian writer Leo Tolstoy. (His name in Russian is Л. Н. Толстой, and five of the nine letters in his name are now familiar to you.)

Сказка	*A Fairy Tale*
"КТО СИДЕЛ НА МО–ЁМ СТУЛЕ И СДВИНУЛ ЕГО С МЕСТА?"	"WHO'S BEEN SITTING ON MY CHAIR AND MOVED IT OUT OF PLACE?"

"кто сидел на моём стуле   "who's been sitting on my
. . .?"   chair . . .?"

"Кто сидел на моём стуле   "Who's been sitting on my
                                   chair
и сдвинул его с места?"   and moved it out of place?"

Look closely at the Russian dialogue on the left.   Find
the letters Е, З, С.

Read a few words:

    сказка (skahz-ka) — *a fairy tale*

    с (s) — *from,* or *out of*

    с места (s мен-sta) — *out of place;* the word for *place*
      without a preposition in front of it is "место."

Looking again at the eight Russian letters we now know,
we will make up some more simple words.

а е з к м о с т

1   за (zah) — a common preposition, meaning *be-*
      hind, or *onto,* as in *holding onto*

2   заметка (zah-мент-ka) — *a notice,* or *a note* (this
      is our first three-syllable word)

3   замок (zah-мawk) — *a lock*

4   казак (kah-zaнк) — *cossack,* an Americanized
      Russian word, a people in the southern part of
      the Soviet Union, known as expert horsemen

5   касса (kaнs-sa) — *a cashier's booth,* or *a ticket
      office,* or *a box office,* or *cash.* (The Russians,
      who have to translate this one word "касса"

so many different ways into English, think *English* is a very complicated language!)

6   коза (ka-ZAH) — *a female goat*

7   комета (kah-MEH-ta) — *comet*

8   коса (ka-SAH) — *a braid, as a braid of hair*

9   масса (MAHS-sa) — *a mass* or *lot, as a lot of people; or bulk*

10   места (meh-STAH) — *places*

11   место (MEH-sto) — *place*

12   моет (MO-yeht) — *washes* (verb)

13   мост (mawst) — *bridge*

14   оса (aw-SAH) — *wasp;* ос (aws), plural following a numeral

15 остаток (ahs-TAH-tok) — *remainder,* or *leftover*

16 с (s) — besides being a preposition *from* (as in the "Fairy Tale"), с is also a preposition meaning *with.* (A useful preposition!)

17 сам (sahm) — *himself* (pronoun)

18 сама (sah-MA) — *herself* (pronoun)

19 сок (sawk; rhymes with *talk,* or the Russian "ток") — *juice*

20 сто (sto) — the numeral *one hundred;* notice that it has two letters from the English word *century*

21 тема (TYEH-ma) — *theme,* as *the theme of the story*

22 тесто (TYEH-sto) — *dough*

23 тост (tawst) — *toast* (as in *proposing a toast*)

Had you guessed that you would be able to read that many separate words from only eight letters? If you are not tired of this word game, try by yourself to make some shorter Russian words from two long words you have learned, "заметка" and "остаток."

For further practice in reading words, find Russian rhymes for:

тост

касса

тесто

сам

сок

In spite of the large number of Russian words you can now read and understand, you cannot yet construct sensible sentences, because the words you have learned — except for моет, a verb — are mostly nouns.

You have, however, learned a few pronouns — кто, сам, сама, то, тот; a few prepositions — о, от, с, за; some adverbs — там, так, как; one numeral — сто; and you have seen that the verb *to be* is silent in Russian in the present tense. The other words you know are all nouns. (To find out how difficult it is to make sentences with twenty-five nouns and one verb, try doing it with English words!)

The best we can do in Russian with those words is to make a few brief phrases and questions, and only a couple of real sentences. Trying to use words meaningfully, we will learn about translation.

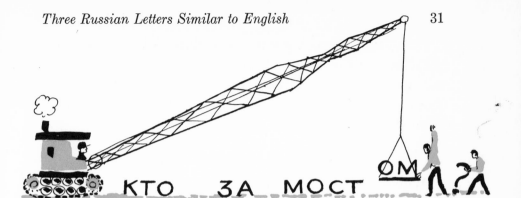

"Кто за мостом?"

Here, the preposition "за" requires the "ом" ending on the masculine noun "мост." It would be just as wrong in Russian to say "Кто за мост?" as it would be wrong (and crude) English to say *Who behind bridge?* The *correct* English translation is: *Who is behind the bridge?* — although there is no *is* and no *the* in the Russian.

From the words we have, we can give an answer which is not too absurd:

"Там за мостом сто ос!"

The plural of "оса" (*wasp*) is required by the word "сто," so we have "ос." The best English translation would be not word for word (*There behind bridge hundred wasps*), but: *There are a hundred wasps behind the bridge.*

Learning to translate Russian into English means not just changing each *word* from Russian to English, but constructing a good English phrase or sentence in place of the good Russian one.

We are also learning some grammar: we have seen that Russian nouns change their endings when used with a preposition, as well as in changing from singular to plural form.

Now watch a noun change its ending in another sentence:

"Кто моет кота?"

We see that the masculine singular noun, "кот," ends here with *a* — this is required by the verb "моет."

The answer to the above question could be:

"Кот сам."

In another sentence, "Там масса теста!" (*There is a mass of dough there!* Or: *There is a lot of dough!*) the noun "тесто" changes its ending and becomes "теста," because the word "масса," *lòt*, in front of it, *implies* a preposition, *of*.

A good way to practice the Russian words you can now read is to arrange the nouns and the pronouns by gender — masculine, feminine, neuter.

Place in one column the masculine words — those ending with a consonant; in another the feminine words — those ending with *a*; and in a third column put the neuter words (all ending with *o*).

In the next chapter, we will learn more letters, more words, more verbs — and soon be able to read sentences.

Chapter 4

Four Russian Letters
That Only LOOK like English

В в   Н н   Р р   У у

All four letters — В Н Р У — look exactly like English ones in the design of capital letters, but they never *sound* the same.

В — called "Veh" — is pronounced *v* (as in *victor*)
Н — called "Enn" — is pronounced *n* (as in *no*)
Р — called "Err" — is pronounced *r* (as in *Russian*)
У — called "Oo" — is pronounced *oo* (as in *poor, tour*)

You now know twelve Russian letters. Here they are in alphabetical order:

А   В   Е   З   К   М   Н   О   Р   С   Т   У

Those twelve letters, particularly the letter Р (*R*), could give us dozens of new words on different subjects. But we would get lost in too many words! We need some plan.

Our plan in this chapter is to concentrate on one subject

at a time. First, we'll learn a number of Russian geographic words. With them, we'll get to know the names
of some places on land and areas of water in the country
where Russian is spoken. Then we will learn and use some
words having to do with weather and time. We'll end the
chapter with a quiz.

Here is a list of some general geographic words, and names
of places you can find on the map:

восток (vah-STAWK) — *east*

карта (KAHR-ta) — *map*

море (MAW-reh) — *sea* (it may remind you of *marine*)

озеро (O-zyeh-ro) — *lake*

океан (a-keh-AHN) — *ocean*

остров (OH-strov) — *island*

река (reh-KA) — *river*

север (SYEH-vehr) — *north*

советское (sa-VYEHT-sko-yeh) — *Soviet,* pertaining to
Soviet Union, as *Soviet geography* (an adjective;
therefore, in Russian, not capitalized)

страна (strah-NA) — *country*

Азовское море (A-ZAWV-sko-yeh MAW-reh) — *the Sea
of Azov*

АССР (Ah Ess Ess Err) (ASSR) — *Armenian
Soviet Socialist Republic*

Кавказ (Kahv-KAHZ) — *the Caucasus,* region in the
Soviet Union

Карское море (Kahr-sko-yeh maw-reh) — *the Kara Sea*

Курск (Koorsk) — *Kursk*, a city

Москва (Mosk-va) — *Moscow*, the capital city of USSR

Мурманск (Moor-MAHNSK) — *Murmansk*, city
река Амур (reh-KA A-MOOR) — *the Amur River*
река Москва (reh-KA Mosk-VA) — *the Moskva River*
река Нева (reh-KA NYEH-va) — *the Neva River*
Ростов (Ros-TAWV) — *Rostov*, a city
Саратов (Sah-RAH-tov) — *Saratov*, a city
Севан (Syeh-VAHN) — *Sevan*, a lake in Armenia
СССР (Ess Ess Ess Err) — USSR
УССР (Oo Ess Ess Err) (USSR) — *Ukrainian Soviet
Socialist Republic.*

In order to talk about these different Russian places you
have now seen on the map, you will need to learn a few
more helpful words:

а (ah) — either *and* or *but*
в (v) — *in*, as *in Moscow*
вот (vawt) — *here is, and here's*
все (vsyeh) — *everybody*
какое (kah-KO-yeh) — *which?*
на (nah) — *on*, as *on the map; to*, as *to the north*
не (nyeh) — *not*, as *The lake is not on the map*
нет (nyeht) — *no*, to indicate a denial
нету (NYEH-too) — *There isn't any* or *aren't any*, or
    don't have any (sometimes нет can also be used)
но (no) — another word for *but*
он (awn) — *he*
она (a-NAH) — *she*
совсем (sahv-SYEHM) — *entirely, completely*

туда (too-DA) — *there, that place*

тут (toot) — *here* (opposite of там)

у (oo) — *by* or *with;* as у нас — *with us,* as in *"It's different with us"*

Some useful nouns:

астроном (ah-stro-NOHM) — *astronomer*

курорт (koo-RAWRT) — *resort*

сестра (syeh-STRAH) — *sister*

стена (styeh-NAH) — *wall*

Some Russian names:

Анна Котова (AHN-na Kah-TAW-va) — *Anna Kotova*

Антон Котов (Ahn-TAWN Kah-TAWV) — *Anthony Kotov*

Варвара Котова (Vahr-VAH-ra Kah-TAW-va) — *Barbara Kotova*

Two special phrases:

у вас (oo vahs) — *you have* (literally, *with you*)

у нас (oo nahs) — *we have* (literally, *with us*)

Unlike the English, Russian words have a way of changing their endings following a preposition, as we have already seen. For example, in English you say "the country" and "in the country," with the noun "country" remaining the same. In Russian you say "страна" and "в стране."

Remembering all this, you will be able to read and understand these simple comments about Russian geography:

У вас на стене карта С С С Р. На север от С С С Р[1] — океан. На севере С С С Р,[2] Карское море. А какое озеро на севере? У нас в стране масса озеров, но тут на карте озеров нету. На карте нету острова. Река Нева на севере, река Амур на востоке, река Москва в Москве.

Антон Котов — астроном. Он на севере, в Мурманске; сестра, Варвара Котова на курорте, а сестра Анна Котова в Саратове. Саратов на востоке от У С С Р. А озеро Севан в У С С Р? Нет. Озеро Севан в А С С Р.

[1] На север от С С С Р — means *to the north of the USSR*
[2] На севере С С С Р — means *in the north (northern) USSR*

You have probably noticed that in Russian you capitalize words differently from English: "Карское море" is correct Russian, although *Kara Sea* is correct English. Proper adjectives are not capitalized: "советское море" is correct Russian, just as *a Soviet sea* is correct English.

You must have also noticed that a last name has different endings for male and female: Anna's last name is "Kotova," while her brother Anthony's name is "Kotov." So in Russian you can usually tell by the last name whether a person is a boy or a girl. In English a brother and a sister would of course have exactly the *same* last name, whether Smith or Kotov; in English you cannot tell by the last name alone whether the person is a boy or a girl; you have to add *Miss* or *Mr.*, or the first name.

Words pertaining in general to time, time of year and weather:

в марте (v MAHR-teh) — *in March* (names of months are *not* capitalized in Russian)
весна (vehs-NAH) — *spring*
ветер (VEH-tyehr) — *wind*
воет (VO-yeht) — *howls*
встанем (vSTAH-nyehm) — *we will get up*

встанет (vstah-nyeht) — *he* or *she will get up*

завтра (zahv-tra) — *tomorrow*

завтрак (zahv-trahk, the same word as *tomorrow*, with
a *k* added) — *breakfast*

комната (kawm-na-ta) — *room*

мороз (mah-roz) — *frost*

рано (rah-no) — *early*

рано утром (rah-no OO-trom) — *early in the morning*

свет (sveht) — *light* (noun)

темно (tyehm-no) — *dark*

утро (OO-tro) — *morning*

We have enough words now for a short discussion on the
subject of March:

Завтра весна.

У нас в марте морозу нет.

Рано утром в комнате свет.

Кто встанет завтра рано?

Все встанем рано на завтрак.

А у нас в марте на реке мороз.   У озера ветер воет.
Утром у нас совсем темно.

Не встанем рано!

In translating the Russian, remember that "is" is understood.   For instance, "Завтра весна" means *tomorrow (is) spring.*

Remember, too, that the peculiarly Russian expression "у нас" cannot be translated with *exact* English words.

In translating you could change *With us in March no frost* to *There is no frost in March here,* or *We have no frost in March.*   For the second sentence with "у нас," we would change the Russian sentence to *But in March we do have frost on the river.*

In the next sentence with "у нас," the English translation is different again: *Here, it is completely dark in the morning.*

The twelve Russian letters which we are using in this chapter will enable us to change the subject after we learn a few additional words:

ваза (VAH-za) — *vase*

окно (awk-NO) — *window*

самовар (sah-mo-VAHR) — *samovar*, a Russian urn for boiling water for tea; not often seen now.

стакан (stah-KAHN) — *glass*, as *glass of water*

тесно (TYEH-sno) — *crowded*

Using these last five words as well as others, we will end this chapter with a quiz. Choose ONE word, from the three words listed below each sentence, to complete it.

В комнате мама, Антон, Варвара, Анна, ——; там тесно.

> страна
>
> стакан
>
> сестра

На стене ——.

> карта
>
> март
>
> тесто

У окна ——.

> оса
>
> весна
>
> касса

На завтрак у нас какао, ——.

    сок

    ваза

    стена

Remember many Russian nouns end according to gender (masculine with a consonant, feminine with *a*, and neuter with *e* or *o*). As you did in the last chapter, find among the word lists masculine, feminine and neuter nouns.

Chapter 5

Six Russian Letters That Have
the Same Sounds as English Letters

Б б　　Г г　　Д д　　Л л　　П п　　Ф ф

These letters, which look so different from English ones, have nevertheless perfectly familiar sounds to us — *b, g, d, l, p, f.*

Б б — called "Beh" — pronounced *b* as in *brother,* "брат" (braht — almost like "brat") in Russian

Г г — called "Geh" — pronounced *g* as in *globe,* "глобус" (GLAW-boos) in Russian. (Occasionally, like the English *g,* г changes its regular sound.)

Д д — called "Deh" — pronounced *d* as in *doctor,* "доктор" (DOHK-tawr) in Russian

Л л — called "Ell" — pronounced *l* as in *lamp,* "лампа" (LAHM-pa) in Russian

П п — called "Peh" — pronounced *p* as in *parade,* "парад" (pah-RAHD) in Russian

Ф ф — called "Eff" — pronounced *f* as in *flag,* "флаг" (flahg) in Russian

You now know eighteen Russian letters, and here they are in alphabetical order. Can you give them their correct sounds?

А Б В Г Д Е З К Л М Н О П Р С Т У Ф

As you can imagine, that many letters would give us many times the number of words we already know; but without more experience with the language and grammar, they would not mean much. So let's select groups of words which belong to one subject, and try to use them.

Begin with geography again.

Proper names:

Белое море (Byeh-lo-yeh maw-reh) — *the White Sea*

Волга (Vol-ga) — *the Volga River*

Десна (Dyehs-na) — *the Desna River*

Днепр (Dnyehpr) — *the Dnieper River*

Европа (Yeh-vro-pa) — *Europe*

Егор (Yeh-gawr) — *Igor* (man's name)

Одесса (O-dyehs-sa) — *Odessa*, a city

Полтава (Pol-tah-va) — *Poltava*, city in Soviet Union

РСФСР (Err Ess Eff Ess Err) (RSFSR) — *Russian Soviet Federated Socialist Republic*, the largest of the fifteen Republics

Северное море (Syeh-vehr-no-yeh maw-reh) — *the North Sea*

Урал (Oo-rahl) — the Ural region of the USSR

Verbs:

будет (воо-dyeht) — *will be,* when used with *he, she*
or *it,* or any singular noun.   Thus we see the verb
"to be" is used, but for the FUTURE TENSE.   Sometimes this verb is used alone — with the pronoun
only implied.   Thus, if someone asks: "Will you be
home tonight?"   Your answer ("Yes, I shall be")
in Russian is "Да, буду" (Dah, воо-doo) — which
says simply, "Yes, shall be" with "I" implied.
This is true of other verbs as well.

дал (dahl) — *(he) gave*

дала (dah-LA) — *(she) gave*

думает (DOO-ma-yeht) — *thinks*

едет (YEH-dyeht) — *goes,* or *going* — but by some
transportation, not on foot

задал вопрос (zah-DAHL vah-PROS) — *asked a question*

работает (rah-воо-ta-yeht) — *works*

смотрел (sma-TREHL) — *(he) looked*

смотрела (sma-TREH-la) — *(she) looked*

Adverbs:

где (gdyeh) — *where?*

далеко (dah-lyeh-ко) — *far*

потом (pa-TOME) — *then*

туда (too-DAH) — *there*

Pronouns:

ero (yeh-VO) — *his.*   (Notice that г (*g*) here has a *v*
sound, instead of *geh.*)

оно (aw-NO) — *it*

Adjective:

прекрасно (preh-KRAHS-no) — *splendid*

Nouns (you can now tell which are masculine, feminine or neuter by the endings):

вопрос (vah-PROS) — *question* (noun)
гора (gaw-RAH) — *mountain*
город (GO-rod) — *city*
города (gaw-ro-DAH) — *cities*
дом (dawm) — *house* or *home*
дома (do-MAH) — *houses*
дома (DAW-ma) — *at home*
запад (ZAH-pahd) — *west*
лето (LYEH-to) — *summer*
летом (LYEH-tawm) — *in summertime,* or *during summer,* or *in the summer*
ответ (at-VYEHT) — *answer* (noun)
поездка (pa-YEHZD-ka) — *trip*

Something to read, with attention to verbs:

Егор смотрел на карту, а его сестра смотрела на глобус. Егор смотрел на запад, на УССР. Там он смотрел на реку Днепр, на реку Десну. Потом он смотрел на города — Одессу, Полтаву. Сестра смотрела на север — на Белое море. Она думает о поездке на север.

Егор задал вопрос, а его сестра дала ответ.

Вопрос: "Где Северное море?"

Ответ: "Северное море не в СССР — оно на севере в Европе, у океана."

Вопрос: "А какое море на севере в РСФСР?"

Ответ: "Там Белое море."

Вопрос: "Кто едет на курорт в Одессу?"

Ответ: "Антон туда едет. Там летом прекрасно."

Вопрос: "А куда едет его сестра Варвара?"

Ответ: "Она будет дома, но она работает не далеко от курорта на Днепре."

Notice that the word "a," used twice in the middle of a sentence and twice at the beginning, means *and*.

As you see, eighteen Russian letters do give us a world of words! Eighteen English letters would, too. But we need still more to have a few lines of conversation about weather, a boat trip and an invitation to dinner.

The new words in the following list are arranged in order of their appearance in the conversation that follows.

разговор (rahz-ga-VOR) — *conversation*

погода (pa-GO-da) — *weather*

у нас (oo nahs) — As we have said, this is hard to translate. It can mean *in our place, by us, with us,* or *we have.*

село (syeh-LO) — *village*

у вас (oo vahs) — *in your place, by you, with you,* also *you have* (as above)

тепло (tyeh-PLO) — *warm*

около (O-kaw-lo) — *near* (preposition)

не так тепло (nyeh tahk tye-PLO) — *not so warm,* or *not quite so warm*

после (PAW-slyeh) — *after* (preposition)

опасно (aw-PAH-sno) — *dangerous*

совсем не опасно (sahv-SYEHM nyeh aw-PAH-sno) — *not at all dangerous*

малое (MAH-lo-yeh) — *little* (neuter gender)

к нам (k nahm) — *to us,* or *to our home*

по (paw) — *on,* or *along*

к вам (k vahm) — *to you,* or *to your home*

лодка (LOD-ka) — *rowboat*

верно (VYEHR-no) — *You are right;* or *right;* or *yes*

да (dah) — *yes*

среда (sreh-DAH) — *Wednesday* (notice that days of week are *not* capitalized)

в среду (v SREH-doo) — *on Wednesday* (though в usually means *in*) [1]

первого марта (PEHR-va-go MAHR-ta) — *on the first of March* (Mar. 1 = первое марта)

тогда (tahg-DAH) — *then*

будете (BOO-dyeh-tyeh) — *you will*, whether you speak to many people, or, in the polite form, to one person

суббота (soob-BO-ta) — *Saturday*

в субботу (v soob-BO-too) — *on Saturday*

не могу (nyeh ma-GOO) — *(I) can't*

могу (ma-GOO) — *(I) am able to,* or *(I) can*

обед (ah-BEHD) — *dinner*

к обеду (k ah-BEHD-oo) — *to dinner* (though *k* usually means *on*)

---

[1] Заметка (NOTE): Remember that the little one-letter prepositions, "о," "в," "с," and others, like "на," in front of a word, change that word's ending.

РАЗГОВОР О ПОГОДЕ

"У нас в селе тепло.   А как у вас около озера?"

"У нас около озера не так тепло."

"А у нас после марта мороза нету — совсем тепло. А на озере не опасно?"

"Нет — совсем не опасно. Оно малое. К нам все едут по озеру."

"А как едут к вам — на лодке?"

"Верно! На лодке. А у вас лодка будет?"

"Да, лодка будет готова в среду, первого марта."

"Тогда, будете у нас в среду?"

"Нет, в среду не могу."

"А в субботу?"

"В субботу могу."

"К обеду?"

"Да, к обеду!"

The word "a" — *and* — is used in this conversation the same way as in the earlier section with dialogue, to balance as well as to connect.

We can now have another conversation — about a dog.
Here are the new words we will need:

о собаке (aw sa-BAH-keh) — *about a dog*

газета (gah-ZYEH-ta) — *newspaper*

Правда (PRAHV-da) — name of a well-known Soviet
    Russian newspaper, *Truth*

рассказ (rahs-SKAHZ) — *story*

как зовут (kahk za-VOOT) — *What is the name of?* or
    What do they call?

одну (a-DNOO) — *one*, feminine (ending "у" agreeing
    with the verb.   In the usual case, feminine *one* is
    "одна.")

белка (BYEHL-ka) — *a squirrel*, also a dog's name

собака (sa-BAH-ka) — *dog*, female

стрелка (STRYEHL-ka) — *Little Arrow*, used as a fe-
    male dog's name

обе (O-byeh) — *both*, feminine

ракета (rah-KEH-ta) — *rocket*

космонавт (kos-mo-NAVT) — *cosmonaut*

космос (KOS-mos) — *cosmos, space*

луна (loo-NA) — *moon* (think of the word *lunar*)

на луне (na loo-NYEH) — *on the moon*

Марс (Mahrs) — *Mars*, planet

будут (BOO-doot) — *(they) will be*

обратно (aw-BRAHT-no) — *on a return trip*

планета (plah-NYEH-ta) — *planet*

знаете (ZNA-yeh-tyeh) — *you know*

откуда знаете? (at-KOO-da ZNA-yeh-tyeh) — "From

where you know?" — *How do you know?* or *Where did you learn this?*

все знаем (vsyeh ᴢɴᴀ-yehm) — *we all know*

героев (geh-ʀo-yehv) — *(of the) heroes, the heroes':* the "ев" ending goes with "поездка," meaning *the heroes' trip*

браво (ʙʀᴀʜ-vo) — *bravo*

РАЗГОВОР О СОБАКЕ

"У нас в Москве газета 'Правда.' В газете рассказ о собаке."

"А как зовут собаку?"

"Одну собаку зовут 'Белка' . . ."

"Белка? Белка не собака!"

"Верно. Белка не собака, но собаку ЗОВУТ 'Белка.'"

"Да, да."

"Так . . . ОДНУ собаку зовут 'Белка,' а одну 'Стрелка' — обе будут на ракете далеко, далеко в космосе."

"Как далеко? На луне? На Марсе?"

"Нет, нет, нет! Там не будут. После космоса — обратно на планету к нам."

"Верно? Откуда знаете?"

"Все знаем о поездке собак героев — вот рассказ тут в газете."

"Да, да. Браво, Белка! Браво, Стрелка!"
"Браво, браво!"

"A Conversation about a Dog" was strictly informal,
and of course limited in vocabulary, but we have been able
to talk about the space trip taken by the Russian dogs.

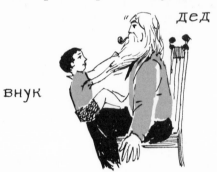

Now we turn to another subject: "At Home." Here
are the new words you will learn, as they appear in the
story:

послезавтра (paw-slyeh-zAHv-tra) — *the day after tomorrow*

папа (PAH-pa) — *papa* or *daddy*, the commonly used
word for *father*

дед (dyehd) — *grandfather;* but another longer word
meaning *granddaddy*, and denoting affection —
дедушка (DYEH-doosh-ka) — is more commonly
used than this word.

внук (vnook) — *grandson;* внука (vNOO-ka) — *granddaughter*

Егорка (Yeh-GAWR-ka) — *little Igor,* a diminutive form for the name *Igor* (as *Johnny* is for *John* in English); ка is a common diminutive ending.

много (MNAW-ga) — *much, many,* or *a great deal*

ресторан (res-to-RAHN) — *restaurant*

маме (MAH-meh) — *for mother,* or *to mother*

трудно (TROOD-na) — *difficult,* or *hard*

помогут (pa-ma-GOOT) — *they will help*

суп (soop) — *soup*

салат (sah-LAHT) — *salad*

булка (BOOL-ka) — *white wheat bread,* or *roll* (as different from rye)

масло (MAHS-lo) — *butter;* it also means *oil;* с маслом (s MAHS-lawm) — *with butter*

молоко (mah-lah-KO) — *milk*

кофе (KAW-feh) — *coffee*

немного (nyeh-MNAW-go) — *not much, not many* or *a few, a little*

конфет (kahn-FYEHT) — *of candies*

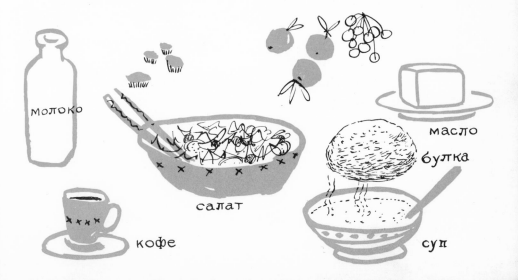

молоко   масло   булка   салат   кофе   суп

самое главное (sᴀʜ-mo-yeh ɢʟᴀʜv-no-yeh) — *the main thing*

фруктов (ғʀᴏᴏᴋ-tav) — *of fruits*

Как вкусно! (kahk vᴋᴏᴏs-no) — *How tasty!*

сказал (skah-ᴢᴀʜʟ) — *(he) said*

деду (ᴅʏᴇʜ-doo) — *for* or *to grandfather*

лет (lyeht) — *years,* when used with *many, how many,* with numerals after *four*

сто лет (sto lyeht) — *a hundred years*

мне (mnyeh) — *to me*

два (dvah) — *two*

два года (dvah ɢᴀᴡ-da) — *two years*

сказала (skah-ᴢᴀʜ-la) — *(she) said*

дадут (dah-ᴅᴏᴏᴛ) — *(they) will give*

подарков (pa-ᴅᴀʜʀ-kov) — *of presents*

красное (ᴋʀᴀʜs-no-yeh) — *red,* with neuter ending

кресло (ᴋʀᴇʜs-lo) — *armchair*

коробка (ka-ʀᴏв-kah) — *box*

табак (tah-вᴀʜᴋ) — *tobacco*

с табаком (s tah-bah-ᴋᴏм) — *with tobacco*

трубка (ᴛʀᴏᴏв-ka) — *a pipe*

радостно (ʀᴀʜ-dast-no) — *happy,* or *glad*

всем (vsyehm) — *to all;* всем будет радостно — *everybody will be happy* or *we'll all be happy*

Now, the story: "At Home."

ДОМА

"Послезавтра у нас все будут на обед: мама, папа, брат, сестра, дед, его внук Егорка, внука Анна."

"Как много! Будет обед в ресторане?"

"Нет, обед будет дома."

"Тогда маме будет трудно."

"Не будет так трудно — маме все помогут."

"На обед у нас будет суп, салат, булка с маслом, молоко, кофе; немного конфет; а самое главное будет много фруктов. Как вкусно!"

После обеда папа сказал: "Завтра деду будет сто лет."

"Мне сто лет," сказал Егорка.

"Егорке два года!" сказала внука Анна.

Деду дадут много подарков: красное кресло, коробку с табаком, трубку. Деду будет радостно.

"Всем будет радостно!" сказал Егорка.

Since the number of new words we learned to read in this chapter is so large, we will learn fewer words in the next chapter — although we will learn nine new letters.

Chapter 6

Nine Russian Letters
That Can Be Spelled Out in English

Ё ё   И и   Й й   Ц ц   Ч ч   Ш ш   Щ щ   Ю ю   Я я

All the nine letters in this chapter look different from English letters. What is more, there are no English letters that sound like these nine Russian letters. However, each one of them can be spelled out by using several English letters, and they can be pronounced easily.

Ё ё is called "Yo" (as in *yoke*). It differs from E e (Yeh) only by the two dots. Those dots are usually omitted in regular print, and Russians just have to KNOW which *e* is pronounced "yeh" and which "yo" — probably much the way Americans know that the same letter, *c*, can sound like *s* (as in *cent*) one time and like *k* (as in *come*) another.

Ё is pronounced "yo" at the beginning of a word, as:

ёлка (YOL-ka) — *a little fir tree, or a Christmas tree*

ёлка

Ё is also pronounced fully, "yo," when it follows a vowel, as:

даёт (dah-YOT) — *gives*
моё (maw-YO) — *my, neuter pronoun*

But after a consonant, ё sounds like "yaw" and seems to make the consonant softer:

всё (vsyaw) — *everything*
котёнок (kah-TYAW-nawk) — *kitten*. (There seems to be as much change in т from "кот" to "котёнок" as in the English *t* from *cat* to *kitten* or *kitty*.)

The vowels е, ё, и, ю, я are called *soft* vowels, because they make consonants sound softer. You will understand this better as you listen to Russian spoken.

Some new words are:

готово (gah-то-vo) — *ready*

к Новому Году (k No-vo-moo GAw-doo) – *for the New
Year* (capitalized because it is a holiday, as in
America)

У нас в комнате будет ёлка.   Всё будет готово
к Новому Году.

И и is called "Ee" and pronounced *ee* as in *meeting*,
which is also a Russian word, "митинг" — pronounced
practically the same, with the same stress.   И is a much-
used soft vowel.

Many plurals of nouns, pronouns and verbs, of all three
genders, are formed by the addition of и:

дети (DYEH-tee) — *children* (neuter)

ёлки (YOL-kee) — *fir trees* (feminine)

мои (mo-EE) — *my,* or *mine,* plural, any gender

они (a-NEE) — sounds like "a knee" — *they* (any gender)

собаки (sa-BAH-kee) — *dogs* (masculine)

сказали (SKAH-zah-lee) — *(they) said*

И often occurs in proper adjectives, such as the following:

американские (ah-meh-ree-KAHN-skee-yeh) — *American* (adj. plural)

русские (ROOS-skee-yeh) — *Russian* (adj. plural)

украинские (oo-krah-EEN-skee-yeh) — *Ukrainian* (adj. plural)

The expression, "Do you speak . . . (a language)?" requires an и after the name of the language:

по американски (paw ah-meh-ree-KAHN-skee) — *in American,* or *American*

по русски (paw ROOS-skee) — *in Russian,* or *Russian*

по украински (paw oo-krah-EEN-skee) — *in Ukrainian,* or *Ukrainian*

И occurs in many Russian names of people and places.

Владимир (Vlah-DEE-meer) — *Vladimir*

Екатерина (Yeh-kah-tyeh-REE-na) — *Catherine*

Иван (Ee-VAHN) — *Ivan;* corresponds to *John*

Ленин   Ленинград

Киев (KEE-yehv) — *Kiev*
Ленин (LYEH-neen) — *Lenin*
Ленинград (Lyeh-neen-GRAHD) — *Leningrad*
Лиза (LEE-za) — *Lisa*
Никита (Nee-KEE-ta) — *Nikita*
Нина (NEE-na) — *Nina*

The letter и by itself is the word most often used for
and.

Now you can read and translate the following two sentences:

Москва и Ленинград русские города, а Миннеаполис и Балтимор американские.

Иван и Лиза мои брат и сестра.   Они едут на
митинг в Киев.

И occurs in many common words. One is:

мир (meer) — *peace* (the same word also means *world*)

Свет (sveht) — *light* — also means *world*. Thus the meaning of "the world" in Russian is touched with *peace* and *light*.

Here are some more new words:

скоро (SKAW-ro) — *soon*
на свете (na SVEH-tyeh) — *in the world*
сказано (SKAH-zah-no) — *(it) is said*
спасибо (spah-SEE-bo) — *thank you*

You can now read and translate the following two sentences by yourself:

Сказали дети, "Скоро на всем свете будет мир."
"Верно сказано — Спасибо."

Next, with the addition of the letters ё and и, we will learn a Russian saying. In Russian, as in other languages, old sayings are often repeated to give you encouragement, or to help you understand something.

Всё идёт как по маслу.

Translated word for word, this means: "Everything is going as if on oil" — in other words, "Everything is going smoothly." Perhaps we can use this saying as encouragement while we learn the next strange Russian letter.

Й has the sound of *y* in *boy;* one can hardly say it by itself; й is a unique letter in the Russian alphabet; it is called "half-a-vowel," and also "short ee." It looks exactly like the и (ee) except for a little curl above the letter but not connected with it.

There are very few words *beginning* with the letter й. The easiest one for you to learn is:

йод (yohd) — *iodine* (It sounds somewhat like the middle syllable of the English word.)

Й occurs commonly in Russian speech, however — notably in masculine names:

Алексей (Ahl-yehk-sᴇʜʏ) — *Alexis*
Андрей (Ahn-ᴅʀᴇʜʏ) — *Andrew;* rhymes with *day*
Григорий (Gree-ɢᴀᴡ-reey) — *Gregory;* rhymes with story
Николай (Nee-kaw-ʟᴀʏ) — *Nicholas;* rhymes with *sky*
Сергей (Sehr-ɢᴇʜʏ) — *Sergei*

Й is also used on the end of masculine pronouns and adjectives in the singular form.

американский (ah-meh-ree-ᴋᴀʜɴ-skeey) — *American*
великий (vyeh-ʟᴇᴇ-keey) — *great*
Великий Океан (Vyeh-ʟᴇᴇ-keey O-keh-ᴀʜɴ) — *the Pacific Ocean*

Николай

Левь Толстой

мой (moy)— *mine* or *my*
русский (ʀoos-skeey) — *Russian*

You should have no difficulty reading and translating
the following three phrases, containing three Russian
words you have not seen before.

Мой внук Андрей тут на фотографии.
Левь Толстой — великий русский автор.
Вен Клайборн — американский пианист.

Й occurs in the middle of many common words. One
of them you will have no difficulty in learning. It is:

тройка (ᴛʀoʏ-ka) — *troika, a team of three horses*

But another (perhaps the most common of Russian words!) may be troublesome at first. This long word is:

Здравствуйте! (ᴢᴅʀᴀʜsт-vooy-tyeh) — *How do you do?* or *Hello!*

This everyday Russian greeting is perfectly correct for use with strangers or elders or important people, yet it is not really quite as formal as "How do you do?" in English. "Здравствуйте" is also a common, friendly greeting, but not quite as casual as "Hello!" It may take some practice to learn this long Russian word, in which the first в (*v*) is silent. It is an old word, the root of which, "здрав," means *good health*. (And this gives a nice feeling to a greeting word, in whatever language!)

Здравствуй! (ᴢᴅʀᴀʜsт-vooy) — *Hi!* — is the same greeting in the singular form, used with intimate friends or family, or when addressing *one* child. So we say:

"Здравствуй, Егорка!"
"Здравствуйте, дети!"

Ц ц (called "Tseh") is pronounced somewhat as *ts* in *it's*, when you say it fast (*"It's hot here!"*). It also sounds like the second *c* in the English word *concert*, which is the same word in Russian — "концерт" (kahn-тѕеннт).

Here are other common words in which ц appears:

цвет (tsvyeht) — *flower*, also *color*
цена (tsyeh-NAH) — *price*, or *value*

центр (tsehntr) — *center*
цирк (tseerk) — *circus*

Ц is often used at the end of masculine proper nouns, as:

американец (ah-meh-ree-KAH-nyehts) — *(male) American*
африканец (ah-free-KAH-nyehts) — *(male) African*
иностранец (ee-na-STRAH-nyehts) — *(male) foreigner;* literal meaning of the word is *"one from another country."*
украинец (oo-krah-EE-nyehts) — *(male) Ukrainian*

The word for *male Russian*, however, does not have the same ц ending: "русский" means *Russian* both as a masculine noun and as an adjective.

Try changing the Russian words for *American, Ukrainian, African* and *foreigner* from masculine to feminine, by taking away the last two letters on each word and adding "-ка" (keeping the same stress).

Now read the following paragraph containing many words with the letter ц. There will be only a few words not already familiar to you:

праздник (ᴘʀᴀʜᴢ-dneek) — *holiday*
весело (ᴠᴇʜ-syeh-lo) — *gay, fun*
пойдём (pay-ᴅʏᴏᴍ) — *we are going to go*
давно (dahv-ɴᴏʜ) — *long ago, once upon a time*
ни (nee) — *neither*, or *nor*

Завтра у нас праздник. В городе будет парад, будет много флагов, много цветов. Будет весело! Все пойдём в город — но ни на парад, ни в театр, ни в цирк — а на концерт. Завтра американец Вен Клайборн даёт концерт у нас в Киеве. Не так давно он играл в Москве.

Ч ч is called "Cheh" as in *check*, and looks a little like an upside-down chair. Many common Russian words have ч in them. For example:

потому что (pa-ta-мoo shto) — *because*
почему? (pa-cheh-мoo) — *why?*
почта (pawch-ta) — *mail*
ученик (oo-cheh-neek) — *pupil, or student*
чай (chay) — tea; на чай — *to tea,* or *for tea;* chay
   rhymes with *shy*
чайник (chay-neek) — *teapot,* for brewing tea
часто (chah-sto) — *often, frequently*
человек (cheh-lo-vehk) — *a man,* or *a human being*
читали (chee-тah-lee) — *(they) have read* (past tense)
что? (shto) — *what?* (Here is an exceptional pronunciation of ч; *sh* instead of *ch.*)

There are seven new words in the next exercise:

класс (klahss) — needs no translation
из (eez) — *from*
ему (yeh-мoo) — *(to) him*
интересно (een-tyeh-rehs-no) — needs no translation
вода (va-dah) — *water*
кипит (kee-peet) — *is boiling*
пригласите (pree-gla-see-tyeh) — *(you) invite*

Кто тот человек — он в классе с учениками? Он иностранец из Африки. Он ученик.
Почему он у нас? Потому что ему интересно.

А чай готов? Да, готов. Вот чайник, и вода
кипит в самоваре. Пригласите африканца.

Ч appears also in many Russian names of places and
people:

>Чайковский (Chay-конv-skeey) — *Tchaikovsky* (the
>   composer)
>
>Чёрное море (Снонr-no-yeh мaw-reh) — *the Black
>   Sea*
>
>Снегурочка (Snyeh-гoo-rach-ka) — *the Snow Maiden*
>   (in the Russian folktale)
>
>Сочи (Сoн-chee) — *Sochi*, a Black Sea resort town

Чайковский великий русский композитор.
Американские дети часто читали сказку "Снегурочка," но они не читали по русски, они читали
сказку по английски.

You can translate for yourself the phrase "по английски."

Снегурочка

One hears the letter ч most frequently, in the Russian language, when it makes a diminutive form.

Here are some nouns you already know changed to their diminutive forms by use of the letter ч.

внук . . . внучек (vNOO-chek)

внука . . . внучка (vNOOCH-ka)

вода . . . водичка (vah-DEECH-ka)

коробка . . . коробочка (ka-RO-bach-ka) — *a box . . . a little box*

кот . . . котик, котичек (KAW-teek, KAW-tee-chek) — *kitten, or "kitty"*

лампа . . . лампочка (LAHM-pach-ka)

лодка . . . лодочка (LO-dach-ka)

мама . . . мамочка (MAH-mach-ka) (*little mother* is sometimes used for "*mother dear*")

папа . . . папочка (PAH-pach-ka)

самовар . . . самоварчик (sah-mo-VAHR-cheek)

сестра . . . сестричка (syeh-STREECH-ka) — *a little sister*

трубка . . . трубочка (TROO-bach-ka)

чайник . . . чайничек (CHAY-nee-chek)

The frequent use of diminutives in Russian speech has a special meaning, hard to explain. For example: a grownup asking for a drink of water would ask: "Дайте мне водички!" This wouldn't exactly mean he *wanted* only *a little bit of water*. It would imply a pleasantness in the asking, as with the English phrase: "May I have *a little water*, please?" Here is another example: a lady may refer to her granddaughter as "внучка," *little grand-daughter*, even if the granddaughter is really quite big; "внучка" sounds much softer than "внука."

The regular word for *girl* in Russian is a diminutive: "девочка" (DYEH-vach-ka); also that for *butterfly*, which is "бабочка" (BAH-boch-ka).

The use of ч is frequent in names. If a girl "Нина" is your friend, or if Nina is a child, you will probably call her "Ниночка" (NEE-nach-ka). And if your friend were named "Анна," you'd call her "Аннечка"; and if the friend were "Егор" (whom we called "Егорка" before), you might call him affectionately "Егорчик" or "Его-рочка."

Thus, when you use a diminutive ending on a name in Russian, you don't need the word *little;* sometimes it also takes the place of *dear.*

Ч is also used as the last of three letters ending Russian male middle names, to show that the man is *the son of* somebody. What an indispensable letter is ч!

Here are a few Russian middle names for men:

Александрович (Ah-lyehk-SAHN-dro-veech)
Алексеевич (Ah-lyehk-SEH-yeh-veech)
Иванович (Ee-VAH-no-veech)
Петрович (Pyeh-TRO-veech)

The corresponding women's middle names are used with "овна" or "евна": "Ивановна," "Петровна," "Алек-сеевна," "Александровна."

The ending "вна" thus means the woman is *the daughter of*.

There are new words in the following paragraph, and two cities to find on a map (Chernigov and Sochi) as well as two places you may translate for yourself!

из . . . в (eez . . . v) — *out of . . . to*
оттуда (at-тоо-da) — *from there*
поедут (paw-ʏɛн-doot) — *will go, by transportation*
домой (daw-моʏ) — *home*
через (снɛн-ryehz) — *across* (a preposition)

Иван Иванович и его сестра Александра Ивановна едут из города Чернигова в Сочи, на Чёрном море, потом будут в американском городе Чикаго, а оттуда поедут в Чили. Домой в Чернигов поедут по Великому океану, через Северное море.

With two more words —

вечера (vʏɛн-cheh-ra) — *(than the) evening*
мудренее (moo-dreh-нʏɛн-yeh) — *wiser*

— we can now learn a Russian proverb.   As is true of most proverbs, it is very brief!

Утро вечера мудренее (*The morning is wiser than the evening*).

Ⅲ ш is called *Shah*, and pronounced as *sh* in *shore*.   It has a very simple shape — something like a gate with three straight vertical posts.   Like the letter ч, it is very prominent in Russian speech, and it also is indispensable for many common diminutives.

The use of so many diminutives in Russian seems to give a good deal of flexibility to each word.   For example, if you are talking about *a cute little baby bonnet*, you can just say "шапочка" instead of the regular word for *hat*, which is "шапка."   Thus Russian diminutive endings such as "очка" take the place of several extra words that would be needed in English to express littleness, or pleasantness, or affection.

Some words are *always* used in diminutive forms requiring ш, such as:

бабушка   (ВАН-boosh-ka) — *grandmother*   (really "*granny*")

дедушка   (DYEH-doosh-ka) — *grandfather*   (really "*granddaddy*")

крошка (KROSH-ka) — commonly used as an affectionate term for *little child* or *little baby*, but means *crumb*

Some diminutive Russian words, as you have seen already, have no relation to size, but only signify sentiment; such as "матушка" or "мамочка," *mother dear*, said with sentiment or reverence.

The same sense of sentiment applies to many other diminutives in common use with Russian names, in which the letter ш is often used.   We have:

Алёша (Ahl-YO-sha) — familiar form of "Алексей" — *Alex*

Гриша (GREE-sha) — common nickname for "Григорий" — Gregory

Маша (MAH-sha) — a very common diminutive of *Maria*

Миша (MEE-sha) — as common a boy's first name as "Маша" is a girl's; diminutive of *Michael*

Наташа (Nah-TAH-sha) — also a common diminutive, of *Natalie*

Саша (SAH-sha) — diminutive for "Александра," "Александр" — *Alexandra* or *Alexander*

Such forms for first names are used in Russian by family and friends.   In formal communications, and in proper social conduct (including addressing a teacher), one calls

a person by his or her full first name *and* middle name.
This is considered the right Russian way.   Thus, a young
man may be called "Саша" or even "Сашка" (a still
further diminutive) at home, and by old friends, but at
work he would be known as "Александр Владимирович"
if his father's name were "Владимир";   and his mail
would be addressed to him with correct first, middle and
last name.   However, for expediency in signing writing or
printed works, the initials of first and middle name are
entirely acceptable, even for an author's name on his book.

You may think that Russian names, being long and
changeable, are quite complicated, and that by comparison
American names are generally shorter and simpler.   And
you may be right!

Ш is also in С Ш А, Russian form for U S A, and in many
common words:

> каша, кашка (KAH-sha, KAHSH-ka) — *porridge*
> кошка (KAWSH-ka) — *cat* (female)
> напишу (nah-pee-SHOO) — *I will write*
> наш (nahsh) — *our* (masculine)
> нашла, нашёл, нашли (nahsh-LA, nah-SHOL, nahsh-
>   LEE) — *she, he, they found*
> покушаем, покушали (pa-KOO-sha-yehm, pa-KOO-
>   shah-lee) — *we shall eat, they have eaten*
> слушали (SLOO-shah-lee) — *they listened*
> смешно (smesh-NO) — *funny*, or *amusing, causing
>   laughter*

тише (TEE-sheh) — *quieter,* or *be quiet*

ушла, ушёл, ушли (oosh-LA, oosh-YOL, oosh-LEE) —
    she, he, they went, or *went away*

школа (SHKAW-la) — *school*

шум (shoom) — *noise*

шутки (SHOOT-kee) — *jokes;* sing.: шутка (SHOOT-ka)

Ш-ш (sh-sh) — *shush,* or *hush*

With a few more words —

такой (ta-KOY) — *such*

попили (paw-pee-LEE) — *(they) finished drinking*

книгу (KNEE-goo) — *book* (accusative)

про (proh) — *about*

— you can read a sentence about noise, and three sentences about school and reading.

Ш-ш, тише! Почему такой шум в комнате? Всем смешно от шутки.

Дети покушали кашку, попили чай и ушли в школу. В школе дети читали книгу, "Почта" — автора С. Маршака [1] — книгу "Шутки," и рассказ "Про Томку" (рассказ о собаке) — автора Е. И. Чарушина.[1] Потом слушали сказку великого русского автора Пушкина.[1]

---

[1] "a" at the end of the three names with автора means *by: by the author S. Marshak,* etc.

S. Marshak and E. Charushin are well-known contemporary Russian writers of children's stories, and Pushkin is one of the most famous Russian classical writers.

Now a few sentences on a different subject, which will contain two new words:

по какому (paw kah-кон-moo) — *by which . . .?*
маршрут (mahrsh-коот) — *route of travel*

"По какому маршруту едете из города Ташкента в С С С Р — в город Вашингтон в С Ш А?"
"Напишу о таком трудном маршруте утром — утро вечера мудренее."

Щ щ is called "Shchah" and pronounced as *sh-ch* in "fi*sh* *ch*owder" or in "Do you ca*sh* *ch*ecks?" said quickly. It has the same basic shape as ш, but it has a little tail on the right.

Here are some new words — many with щ — so that we can soon talk about having dinner.

товарищ, товарищи (to-VAH-reeshch, to-VAH-ree-shchee) — *comrade, comrades*

обещали (a-byeh-SHCHAH-lee) — *they promised*

прийти, прийдут, пришли (PREEY-tee, preey-DOOT, preesh-LEE) — *to come, they will come, they came*

ещё (yeh-SHCHO) — *still*, or *yet*

ищут (EE-shchoot) — *they are looking for;* ищет (EE-shchyeht) — *is looking for*

сварила (svah-REE-la) — *(she) cooked*

борщ (borshch) — *borsch, a Russian vegetable soup*

овощи (O-va-shchee) — *vegetables*

принесёт (pree-neh-SYAWT) — *(he or she) will bring*

корзинка (kar-ZEEN-ka) — *a little basket*, nom.; корзинку (kar-ZEEN-koo) after verb (accusative)

Мои товарищи обещали прийти на обед, но ещё не пришли. Они ищут наш дом. Мама сварила борщ с овощами [1] а бабушка принесёт корзинку с фруктами.

[1] Note different forms, after " c."

A sentence with two new words and a new phrase:

нищий (NEE-shcheey) — *pauper*
написан (nah-PEE-sahn) — *is written; written by*
его зовут (yeh-VO za-VOOT) — (*he is*) *called,* or *his
name is* (literally, *they call him*)

Рассказ "Принц И Нищий" написан великим американским автором — его зовут Марк Твейн.

Translate the above Russian sentence into English.

Learn four more new words:

нашу (NAH-shoo) — *our* (the singular, feminine form)
своего (svo-yeh-VO) — *her*
говорит (ga-va-REET) — *says*
покормит (pa-KOR-meet) — (*he or she*) *will feed*

Now read something simple about a cat named Moorka (because in Russian a cat purrs "moorr-moorr").

РАССКАЗ О КОШКЕ МУРКЕ

Нашу кошку зовут Мурка. Кошка Мурка ищет своего котёнка. Вот и нашла! "Мр-мр-мр," говорит Мурка и моет своего котёнка. Потом молоком покормит. Котёнку будет тепло.

Notice "кошка" has the *e* ending, "кошке," following the preposition *o,* and the *y* ending, "кошку," with the verb "зовут."

The letter Ю ю — which looks like the numeral 10 connected with a bridge — is called "You." It is pronounced *yu* (as *u* in *humor*) at the beginning of a word, as in the name "Юрий Гагарин" (Yu-reey Gah-GAH-reen), the astronaut; it is also pronounced *yu* when it follows a vowel, as in "союз" (SA-yuz) — *union*.

When ю follows a *consonant*, however, it is pronounced *oo*, as in *too*, but, being a soft vowel, it makes that consonant soft, as in the name "Анюта" (Ah-NYOO-ta) — another diminutive of "Анна."

Ю is a useful letter in Russian grammar, for it is used as a case ending for feminine words:

которую (ka-TOR-oo-yu) — *which*

красивую (krah-SEE-voo-yu) — *pretty*, or *good-looking*

мою (ma-YU) — *my*, when applied to singular feminine noun

новую (NO-voo-yu) — *new*, when used with a verb

свою (sva-YU) — *her own*, or *her*

Ю is also a verb ending for the first person singular, as in:

качаю (kah-CHAH-yu) — (*I*) *rock*, or *am rocking*

любит (LYOO-beet) — *loves*

люблю (lyoo-BLYOO) — (*I*) *love*

пою (pa-YU) — (*I*) *sing*, or *am singing*

With the addition of a few more words —

куколка (кoo-kal-ka) — a diminutive of кукла
(кook-la) — *doll*
поёт (pa-YOT) — *sings*
песенка (PEH-syen-ka) — *song,* diminitive
придумала (pree-DOO-mah-la) — *she made up,* or *she thought up*
баюшки баю (BAH-yu-shkee bah-YU) — (a special
Russian expression for a lullaby refrain) *rockaby* or
lullaby
ей (YEH-y) — (*to*) *him*

you can read this simple composition:

Анюта, наша сестричка, любит свою новую куколку. Она поёт куколке свою красивую песенку,
которую она сама придумала.

"Баюшки баю
Качаю и качаю
Куколку мою.
И куколку люблю
И песню ей пою —
Баюшки баю."

Я я is the last letter in this chapter's group of nine letters which we are able to spell out in English.

Я is called "Yah," and is pronounced "yah" as in *yard*.

It looks like an inverted ʀ. And я alone is the pronoun *I;* but in Russian this word is not conspicuous, because it is not capitalized unless it begins a sentence.

Я пишу по русски но я читаю по английски — *I write in Russian but I read in English*

When я follows a vowel, it has a full "yah" sound, as in:

моя (ma-ʏᴀʜ) — *my* or *mine*
первого мая (ᴘᴇʜʀ-va-go ᴍᴀʜ-yah) — *on the first of May*

We saw it in Charushin's verse, in Chapter 2:

Как приятно (Kahk pree-ʏᴀʜᴛ-no) — *How pleasant . . .*

Я appears as the feminine ending of many educational words:

бактерия (bahk-ᴛʏᴇʜ-ree-yah)
биография (bee-a-ɢʀᴀʜ-fee-yah)
биология (bee-a-ʟᴏ-gee-yah)
география (geh-o-ɢʀᴀʜ-fee-yah)
геология (geh-a-ʟᴏ-gee-yah)
зоология (zaw-o-ʟᴏ-gee-yah)
физиология (fee-zee-a-ʟᴏ-gee-yah)
фотография (fo-to-ɢʀᴀʜ-fee-yah)

бактерия

All those words should be easy to translate into English!

When я follows a consonant it has a *yah* sound, but being a soft vowel it makes the consonant soft; and soft syllables make the whole word soft.   Here are some common soft Russian words:

дитя (dee-TYAH) — *child*

дядя (DYAH-dyah) — *uncle;* may be used to address a strange man, especially by a child.

няня (NYAH-nyah) — *nursemaid*

тётя (TYO-tyah) — *aunt* or *aunty;* may be used to address a strange lady, especially by a child.

Я is an indispensable letter in diminutive names — boys' and girls'.

Катя (KAH-tyah) — diminutive of Екатерина (Yeh-kah-tyeh-REEN-a) — *Catherine*

Коля (KOL-yah) — diminutive of Николай (Nee-kaw-LAY) — *Nicholas*

Петя (Рен-tyah) — diminutive of Пётр (Pyotr) — *Peter*

Соня (Saw-nyah) — diminutive of София (SO-fee-yah) — *Sophia*

Федя (Fen-dyah) — diminutive of Фёдор (Fyaw-dor) — *Theodore*

Я is also an ending for feminine adjectives:

красная шапочка — This phrase says *Red Little Hood.* It is the title for "Little Red Riding Hood."
светлая комната
красивая девочка
популярная книга
американская тётя

All the above words should be familiar.

With one more feminine adjective —

народная (nah-rod-na-yah) — *folk,* or *people's*

we can comment on a book:

"Баба Яга" русская народная сказка. Американские и русские дети читают книгу "Баба Яга." Она популярная книга в нашей стране, США.

With the addition of

приедет (pree-yeh-dyet) — *will arrive*
говорят (ga-va-ryat) — *they say*

we now have a comment on travel:

Дядя уедет в Аляску.[1]   Тётя приедет к нам в гости.   Летом все поедем на курорт в Ялту.   Как приятно!   Говорят что погода там прекрасная.

[1] Заметка: Аляска — американский штат, а Ялта русский город. Они на карте.

We can now use twenty-seven Russian letters! Here
they are in alphabetical order:

А Б В Г Д Е Ё З И Й К Л М Н
О П Р С Т У Ф Ц Ч Ш Щ Ю Я

Read this proverb, which advises you to act instead of
talk:

> Не по словам судят, а по делам. (*They judge —*
> "судят" *— not by words, but by deeds —* "де-
> лам.")

There is a similar — but not *exactly* the same — proverb
in English: "Deeds speak louder than words."

And this tells you when to do what:

> Всякому делу своё время. (*For every kind —*
> "всякому" *— of work there is its own time*
> *—* "время.")

The similar English saying is: "There is a time and
place for everything."

And now is the time for the next chapter.

Chapter 7

Four Russian Letters That Are Difficult
to Spell but Possible to Say in English

Ж ж   Х х   Ы ы   Э э

Ж is called "Zheh." It has the sound of *s* in *pleasure* or *vision*, the sound of *z* in *seizure*, and the sound of *g* in *regime*. But unlike the English *s*, *z* and *g*, which share its sound, the Russian ж always sounds the same, no matter what letters are next to it.

Because of its distinctive shape you should have no difficulty remembering ж. It looks a little like a bug, and in Russian the word for *bug* begins with ж: "жук" (zhook). Here are more words for using the letter ж in learning Russian.

бежим (beh-ZHEEM) — *we are running*

даже (DAH-zheh) — *even*

ждут (zhdoot) — *(they) wait*

Женя, Серёжа (ZHEN-nyah, Seh-RYO-zha), boys' names — as usual, with different forms after different verbs and prepositions

жужжит (zhoozh-ZHEET) — *buzzes,* or *drones*

журнал (zhoor-NAHL) — *a magazine,* or *a journal*

книжка (KNEEZH-ka) — *book,* used as well as книга.

нужна (NOO-zhna) — *needed, necessary* (referring to feminine object)

прибежали (pree-beh-ZHAH-lee) — *came running*

прибежим (pree-beh-ZHEEM) — *we'll come running*

тоже (TO-zheh) — *also*

уже (oo-ZHEH) — *already*

ужин (OO-zheen) — *supper*

Here are some more new words we'll need:

на улице (nah OO-lee-tseh) — *on the street*

темнеет (tyehm-NYEH-yeht) — *it is getting dark*

кроме (KRO-meh) — *besides, except*

пора (pa-RAH) — *it's time*

принёс (pree-NYAWS) — (*he*) *brought*

библиотека (bee-blee-a-TEH-ka) — *library*

Жуки жужжат, на улице темнеет, детей уже на ужин ждут. "Бежим, бежим!" они сказали и прибежали. Все прибежали кроме Жени. "Пора на ужин — без Жени," сказал Серёжа. "Семеро одного не ждут." [1] Но все ждали Женю и скоро он тоже прибежал и даже принёс журнал из библиотеки.

[1] "Семеро одного не ждут" is a proverb, *Seven do not wait for one.*

More easy use of the letter ж:

надежда (nah-DYEHZH-da) — *hope*, also used as a woman's first name

Жуков, Жукова (Zhoo-KAWV, Zhoo-KO-va) — last names.

муж (moozh) — *husband*

жена (zheh-NA) — *wife*

живут (zhee-VOOT) — *they live*

Житомир, город в УССР (Zhee-TO-meer, GAW-rod v Oo Ess Ess Err) — *Zhitomir, a city in the Ukraine*

Париж, город во Франции (Pah-REEZH, GAW-rod vo FRAN-tzee) — *Paris, a city in France*

Надежда Петровна Жукова и Николай Иванович
Жуков муж и жена.   Они живут в городе Житомире
и поедут на визит [1] в Париж.

X x, which looks like the English *x*, is called "Khah"
(as the sound in the word *Khan*, an Eastern ruler).   Its
sound may be produced by gargling without water in the
mouth (the *h* sound being heard more than the *k* at the beginning of words), or producing the first syllable of the
sneezing sound *kher-choo*.   The Russian word for the sound
of laughter is "ха-ха-ха" (kha-kha-kha) and *laughter* is
"хохот" (кно-khot):

"Как смешно — ха-ха-ха!"

Other x words:

мех (mehkh) — *fur*
меховая (мен-kha-va-yah) — *fur,* an adjective
холодно (кно-lad-no) — *cold*
хорошо (kha-ra-sнo) — *good, all right*
хочу (kha-cнoo) — (*I*) *want*

"На улице холодно.   Мне нужна моя меховая
шапка."

"Хорошо," сказала бабушка.

[1] визит (vee-zeet) — Can you translate?

ox (okh) — *Oh!*
плохо (PLO-kho) — *bad*
муха (MOO-kha) — *a fly*
ухо (OO-kho) — *ear*
уходи (oo-kha-DEE) — *go away*

Ох, как плохо — муха в уже!   Уходи, муха, уходи!
Не жужжи.

тихо (TEE-kha) — *quiet*
найти (nay-TEE) — *to find*
что такое (shto tah-ko-yeh) — *what is . . .*
хижина (KHEE-zhee-na) — *cabin*, or *hut*

В библиотеке тихо.   Я хочу найти одну русскую
книжку: "Что такое хорошо и что такое плохо"; и
одну американскую: "Хижина дяди Тома."

чёрного (CHOHR-naw-vo) — *black* (masc.)

хлеб (khlyehb) — *bread* (usually rye bread)

пойду (pay-DOO) — *I am going to go*

кухня (KOOKH-nyah) — *kitchen*

что-то (SHTO-to) — *something*

пахнет (PAHKH-nyeht) — *smells* (when something has a smell)

понюхай (pah-NYOO-khay) — *(you) smell (it)*.   Notice that the words are quite different for different meanings of "to smell."

свежий (SVEH-zheey) — *fresh*

означает (oh-zna-CHA-yet) — *designates,* or *stands for*

Я хочу вкусного чёрного хлеба.   Пойду в кухню. Там что-то хорошо пахнет!   Понюхай свежий хлеб!

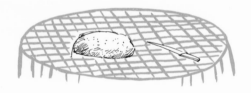

Географическая заметка: СССР означает: Союз Советских Социалистических Республик.

Ы ы, a two-piece letter, most nearly made up of a small b and a Roman I placed close together, is called "Еры" ("Yeri") — which is just a name; it has no sound by itself, for it only occurs following a consonant, at which time it has an *ih* sound, like *i* in *miracle* or *bill.*

Ы is a vowel and is referred to as "the hard и" (ee). It is a common sight and sound in the Russian language.

First, we'll try to distinguish ы from its counterpart, the soft и (ee), as it affects a consonant: In the word "полный" (POL-nihy) — *full* — the н (n) is like the *n* in *niece;* in "ничего" (nee-cheh-vo) — *nothing*, the н (n) is the *n* in *neither*. We also have:

> слышно (SLIHSH-na) — *audible*, and *heard*
>
> сын, сыночек, сынок (sihn, sih-NO-chek, sih-NAWK) — *son, sonny* (the с is like the *s* in *son*)
>
> улыбка (oo-LIHB-ka) — *smile* (the л is like the *l* in *liquid* or *love*)

Compare them with these words with и:

> литература (lee-tyeh-rah-TOO-ra) — *literaturé* (*l* as in *leader*)
>
> синий (SEE-neey) — *blue* (the с is like the *s* in *sea*)
>
> слива (SLEE-va) — plum (*l* as in *leader*)

It is most difficult to distinguish the ы (ih) from the и (ee) following б, в, м, р. This can best be done by listening to and then practicing audible speaking. However, the differences between words with ы and и is very important!

Let's recognize some of them.

> мило (MEE-lo) — *darling, charming, cute*
>
> милый, милая (MEE-liy, MEE-la-yah) — *darling*, masculine and feminine adjectives
>
> мыло (MIH-lo) — *soap*
>
> умыто (oo-MIH-to) — *washed*

With the addition of words . . .

> какая, какое (kah-кан-ya, kah-ко-yeh) — *what* or
> *what a* (fem. and neuter)
> твоё (tva-yo) — *your*, in the informal, singular form
> лицо (lee-тso) — *face*

. . . translate the following sentences, and read the "английская заметка . . ."

> Какая она милая девочка!
> Какое тут мыло в кухне?
> Милый мой сыночек, твоё лицо совсем не умыто.
> В комнате так тихо, ничего не слышно.

АНГЛИЙСКАЯ ЗАМЕТКА О РУССКОЙ ГРАММАТИКЕ!

Remember that the word for *is* is only implied in Russian, so *What she darling little girl* in the first sentence means of course "What a darling little girl she is!"

In the last sentence, the phrase "ничего не слышно" "nothing is *not* heard" is, though double, a *correct* negative in Russian. The Russian phrase for "I don't understand anything" is "Я ничего не понимаю" (literally, *I don't understand nothing*).

The most common words with the vowel ы are the personal pronouns:

вы (vi) — *you* (the *i* as in *vintage*). This is the plural, which is used in all polite social speech even when addressing *one* person. The Russian use of the plural *you* is similar to the English; *you are* is used whether speaking to one person or to many.

ты (ti) — *thou* (the *t* sounds as in *timber*). A singular *you* (or *thou*) used regularly with friends, family and by older people with younger children.

мы (mi) — *we* (the *mi* sound in *miracle*)

Now that you know the sound of ы we will just spell it *i* in English.

Let's see the uses of the words for *you* in Russian. Note the three different adjective endings.

Вы хорошие ученики — *You are good pupils (students).*

Вы хороший ученик, Юрий — *You are a good pupil, Yuri.*

Вы хорошая ученица, Нина — *You are a good pupil, Nina.*

был, была (bil, bi-LAH) — *was (masc. and fem.)*

"Алёшка, мой сынок, где ты был?   И где ты была, Машка?"   (*"Alyoshka, my little son, where have you been?   And where have you been, Mashka?"*)

"Мы тут, мамочка," ответили дети, "а где ты?" (*"We are here, Mommy," answered the children, "and where are you?"*)

The pronoun ты, *you*, *thou*, is also used with animals and with inanimate objects, as here in a children's singsong verse about rain ("little rain" in this form).

Дождик, дождик, не дожди,	Rain, rain, do not rain,
Не дожди ты, подожди.	Do not rain, you, wait (awhile).
Выйди, выйди,[1] солнышко!	Come out, come out, little sun!

[1] "выйди" means "ты выйди"

The most common use of "вы" — *you* — in the polite form is the standard expression for *How are you?*

Here is "Hello! How are you?":

"Здравствуйте! Как вы поживаете?" (pa-zhee-vA-yeh-tyeh)

And the answer, "Fine, thank you, and how are you?":

"Хорошо, спасибо. Как вы?"

The grammatical importance of the letter ы is its use as the ending of many plurals.

Some of these words we have seen already in the singular. Here they are with plurals, and there are some new ones:

буква, буквы (BOOK-va, BOOK-vi) — *letter, letters*
газета, газеты
журнал, журналы
корзина, корзины
пол, полы (pawl, paw-LI) — *floor, floors*
рыба, рыбы (RI-ba, RI-bi) — *fish, fishes*
слива, сливы
стол, столы (stawl, staw-LI) — *table, tables*
ягода, ягоды (YAH-ga-da, YAH-ga-di) — *berry, berries*

Ы can never be used on plurals of words which end with г or к. Thus, on the following words, the и is used:

книга, книги (KNEE-ga, KNEE-gee) — *book, books*

рыбак, рыбаки (ri-ванк, ri-bah-кее) — *fisherman, fishermen*

спутник, спутники (spoot-neek, spoot-nee-kee) — *traveling companion, traveling companions*

Here is a Russian fairy tale title, for you to translate: "Сказка о Рыбаке и Рыбке."

There is another word for *fisherman*: "рыболов" (ri-ba-lov) — literally, *fish-catcher*. And here is another Russian book title: "Советы юному рыболову" ("Advice to a Young Fisherman"). The adjective *to* is expressed by the ending *y* on the words *young* and *fisherman*.

There is also a proverb about fishermen: Рыбак рыбака — видит издалека. ("A fisherman sees [another] fisherman from afar [издалека]" or "One fisherman can always spot another one even from a distance.")

The last in the group of four special Russian letters that are difficult to spell out in English is another hard vowel: Э э ("Eh").

Э — "Eh" — sounds like *e* as in *poet*, which is also a Russian word поэт (pa-ент), with the stress on the last part with э.

Curiously enough, knowing this letter э you can learn a large number of common Russian words with the greatest of ease. Here are a dozen for which no English translation need be given! In each of the Russian words, the sound of э appears identically in the English word.

аэроплан (ah-eh-ro-PLAHN)
аэропорт (ah-eh-ro-PORT)
поэма (pa-EH-ma)
эволюция (eh-va-LYOO-tsee-ya)
экватор (eh-KVAH-tawr)
экзамен (ehk-ZAH-mehn)
экономист (eh-ko-naw-MEEST)
экскурсия (ehks-KOOR-see-yah)
эксперимент (ehks-peh-ree-MEHNT)
электричество (eh-lehk-TREE-chest-vo)
энергия (eh-NEHR-gee-yah)
эхо (EH-kho)

All the words are nouns. Some have the same stressed syllable as the English words, which will help you to learn them.

The most common Russian word with the letter э is "это" — *this*. Here are different forms of it:

это (EH-тo) — *this*, noun neuter, as *this* (*is*): "Это Чёрное море."

эта (EH-ta) — *this*, feminine adjective, as "Эта поэма интересна."

этот (EH-tot) — *this*, masculine adjective, as "Этот американец поэт, его зовут Карл Сэндбург."

эти (EH-tee) — *these*, plural adjective, as "Эти дети не пришли на экскурсию."

A word similar to "это" is "поэтому" (pa-EH-ta-moo) — *therefore* or *because of this*.

Я не понимаю по русски, поэтому я читаю эту книгу.

Since the sound of э is similar to that of e, let's distinguish them — watch the pronunciation:

поэма (pa-EH-ma) — *poem*
поем (pa-YEHM) — *I will eat*

Distinguish the э and e in each sentence.

Я поем ужин, потом прочитаю эту интересную поэму.

Эрик поедет домой.

В Канаде и в Сибири зимой холодно, поэтому там много снега.

зимой (zee-MOY) — *in winter*
снега (SNYEH-ga) — *(of) snow*

In the phrase "я поем ужин," notice that "по" in that verb, as well as in the next sentence, indicates the future tense: *I will eat supper, Eric will go home.*

Also, "про" in front of читаю (I read) is a form of future — *I will read through this interesting poem.* The word "много" — in the phrase "поэтому там много снега" — means both *many* and *much,* or *a great deal,* so the translation here would be: *That is why there is a great deal of snow there.*

Chapter 8

Two Signs Affecting
the Sounds of Letters

Ъ ъ Ь ь

These are special characters in the Russian alphabet:

Ъ called "твёрдый знак" (TVYOR-diy znahk) — *hard sign*

Ь called "мягкий знак" (MYAH-keey znahk) — *soft sign*

Being signs, rather than letters, the ъ and the ь have no sound in themselves. The work of the signs is to give softness or hardness to consonants, at the same time making a slight change in the sound of the vowel:

съеду (s-YEH-doo) — *I'll take a ride,* or *I'll go;* pronounce s-YEH somewhat as in "the book's YEllow pages"

седеть (syeh-DYEHT) — *to grow gray*

съем (s-YEHM) — *I'll eat up;* without the ъ and with a ь at the end, the word would be семь (syehm) — *seven*

The hard sign (ъ) sometimes differentiates one word from a similar one:

въезд (vyehzd) — *arrival*

выезд (vɪ-yehzd) — *departure* (It wouldn't do to confuse those two words!)

Я съеду на станцию. Напишу о выезде из Вашингтона и о въезде в Москву.

We can now learn an important international name, and translate the initials O O H:

Организация (or-gah-nee-zʌн-tsee-yah) — *organization*

Обьединённых (ob-yeh-dee-ɴʏoɴ-nikh) — (of the) *united*

Наций (ɴʌн-tseey) — (of the) *nations*

Observe the difference between

"Соединённые" Штаты Америки — *"United" States of America,* and

Организация "Обьединённых" Наций — *Organization of "United" Nations.*

The word *united* in Соединённые Штаты expresses internal union of smaller parts, while the word *united* in Обьединённых Наций expresses external union of separate nations.

The word for *union* is

союз (sA-yuz), which is the first word of CCCP; "союз" expresses the same idea as "соединённые."

The hard sign, ъ, is the least frequently seen character of the Russian alphabet. In fact, when the sound of the word requires the ъ, it is often legitimately replaced by an apostrophe ('): "Напишу о в'езде в Москву."

The soft sign, ь, is much more functional than its brother; it gets around more and has no substitute. Its unique function is to make a consonant soft, both in the middle and at the end of words. It must be admitted, however, that this special Russian softness of consonants is difficult for non-Russians to detect, or to pronounce. One must learn it by hearing Russian often.

New vocabulary:

о вежливом чижике (aw ᴠᴇʜᴢʜ-lee-vom ᴄʜᴇᴇ-zhee-keh) — *about a polite siskin* (a European bird — finch)

в гости (v ɢᴏs-tee) — *as a guest,* or *for a visit*

чижик (ᴄʜᴇᴇ-zheek) — *siskin,* a quite common European bird, like a finch

прилетел (pree-lyeh-ᴛʏᴇʜʟ) — *(he) flew in*

Ваня (ᴠᴀʜ-nyah) — a boy's name, corresponds to *Johnny*

с клеткой (s ᴋʟʏᴇʜᴛ-koy) — *with a cage*

подбежал (pad-be-ᴢʜᴀʜʟ) — *(he) ran up to*

вежливо (ᴠᴇʜᴢʜ-lee-vo) — *politely*

до свидания (daw svee-ᴅᴀ-nee-ya) — *good-by*

Here is a song, popular with young Russian schoolchildren, which has both *hello* and *good-by* in it.

ПЕСЕНКА О ВЕЖЛИВОМ ЧИЖИКЕ

В гости чижик прилетел,
Прилетел, прилетел:
　"Здравствуй, Ваня!"

Ваня с клеткой подбежал,
Подбежал, подбежал.
Чижик вежливо сказал:
　"До свидания!"

The soft sign ь following a т is the most common ending of verbs in the simple infinitive form.   Try to pronounce the ть softly, as in *kitty*, not *brat*.   The ending corresponds in sound and function to the *to* in an English verb in the infinitive:

вставать (vstah-VAHT) — *to get up*
играть (ee-GRAHT) — *to play*
кушать (KOO-shaht) — *to eat*
писать (pee-SAHT) — *to write*
поговорить (pa-ga-va-REET) — *to have a talk*
понимать (pa-nee-MAHT) — *to understand*
попить (pa-PEET) — *to have a drink*
работать (rah-BOH-taht) — *to work*
спать (spaht) — *to sleep*
учить (oo-CHEET) — *to teach*
читать (chee-TAHT) — *to read*
можете (MOH-zheh-tyeh) — *you can*, or *you may*

Now translate the two lines of verse in Chapter 2:

> Как приятно чай попить,
> О том, о сём поговорить!

Related to the word "учить" is the word "учиться" — (oo-CHEET-syah) — *to learn*, or *to study*, also "научиться" (nah-oo-CHEET-syah) — *to succeed in learning*.   Therefore, "Вы можете научиться по русски" is: "*You can learn Russian.*"

With another new word, you can read comments on this book.

слов (slawv) — *of words*

В этой книге все русские буквы и много русских слов.   Вы будете читать и понимать по русски.

In that simple paragraph the ь appears twice, which shows how often this little "soft" sign is used.   It occurs in all but three of the names of the months, as well as in the word for *calendar*, as you see below.   No English translation is necessary here!

КАЛЕНДАРЬ

январь (yahn-VAHR)
февраль (fev-RAHL)
март (mahrt)
апрель (AH-prel)
май (my)
июнь (ee-YUN)
июль (ee-YUL)
август (AHV-goost)
сентябрь (syehn-TYAHBR)
октябрь (ok-TYAHBR)
ноябрь (no-YAHBR)
декабрь (dyeh-KAHBR)

With the use of the ь, we can learn to count in Russian. Except for три (tree) — 3 — and десять (DYEH-syaht) — 10 — which sound a little like similar English words (*three;*

decimal), the names of the numbers are entirely different from English — until one reaches *a million*, which is мил-лион in Russian.

Here are the basic numbers, 1 to 20; then, we count by tens; then we go by hundreds up to 1000.

1 — один, одна, одно, (a-DEEN, a-DNA, a-DNO) (masc., fem., neuter)

2 — два, две, двое (dvah, dveh, DVO-yeh)

3 — три, трое (tree, TRO-yeh)

4 — четыре (cheh-TI-reh)

5 — пять (pyaht)

6 — шесть (shehst)

7 — семь (syehm)

8 — восемь (VO-syehm)

9 — девять (DYEHV-yaht)

10 — десять (DYEH-syaht)

11 — одинадцать (a-DEE-nahd-tsat)

12 — двенадцать (dveh-NAHD-tsat)

13 — тринадцать (tree-NAHD-tsat)

14 — четырнадцать (cheh-TIR-nahd-tsat)

15 — пятнадцать (pyaht-NAHD-tsat)

16 — шестнадцать (shehst-NAHD-tsat)

17 — семнадцать (syehm-NAHD-tsat)

18 — восемнадцать (vo-syehm-NAHD-tsat)

19 — девятнадцать (dyehv-yaht-NAHD-tsat)

20 — двадцать (DVAHD-tsat)

30 — тридцать (TREED-tsat)

40 — сорок (SO-rawk)
50 — пятьдесят (pyaht-dyeh-SYAT)
60 — шестьдесят (shehst-dyeh-SYAT)
70 — семьдесят (syehm-dyeh-SYAT)
80 — восемьдесят (vo-syehm-dyeh-SYAT)
90 — девяносто (dyehv-yah-NO-sto)
100 — сто (sto)
200 — двести (DVYEH-stee)
300 — триста (TREE-sta)
400 — четыреста (cheh-TI-reh-sta)
500 — пятьсот (pyaht-SAWT)
600 — шестьсот (shehst-SAWT)
700 — семьсот (syehm-SAWT)
800 — восемьсот (vo-syehm-SAWT)
900 — девятьсот (dyehv-yaht-SAWT)
1000 — тысяча (TI-syah-cha)
1,000,000 — миллион (meel-lee-ON)

Note some special features of the Russian arithmetical vocabulary. First, the predominance of the ь in the spelling of numbers. It is sensibly left out in the middle of the words, for 15, 16, 17 and 18; but this character in the Russian alphabet, the ь, does present us with a spelling and phonetic problem in learning the Russian language! Similar sounds, as семь (syehm) and восемь (VO-syehm), look different in 7 and 17, in 8 and 18.

Notice how logical the words for the numbers 20, 30, 50, 60, 70 and 80 are in their relation to 2, 3, 5, 6, 7 and 8.

But then, there is the strange сорок (SO-rawk) for 40 — it has no relation to четыре (cheh-тɪ-reh), 4. But the *hundreds*, as in English, are made up of the word сто, *hundred*, in some form; and 400 is "четыреста," as one might expect.

Notice, too, that the words for *one* and *two* and *three* have different gender endings. This means you say "одна девочка," "один мальчик," "одно дитя" — *one girl, one boy, one child;* "две девочки," "два мальчика," "двое детей" — *two girls, two boys, two children;* "три мальчика, девочки"; "трое детей" — *three boys, girls; three children.* This is quite complicated!

It is interesting to note that the Russian *teen* numbers are from 11, одинадцать — through 19, девятнадцать; while the English *teen* numbers are from 13 through 19.

With the ь we can also read some more proverbs — as usual made up of few words, simple sentences, and good ideas.

Бедность не порок (*Poverty is no vice,* or *Poverty is no crime*).

Что посеешь, то и пожнёшь (*What you sow you'll reap*).

The letter ш is not affected by the soft ь sign; it would still sound *sh* without the ь; but the ь is sometimes there for grammatical verb-ending reasons, as in the word любишь, *you love,* in the next proverb.

Любишь кататься, люби и саночки возить (*You love to go riding, then love to pull the sled. Or, If you love coasting, you have to love to pull your own sled*).

Поспешишь — людей насмешишь   (*When you hurry — you'll make people laugh [at you]. Or, If you hurry too much you'll make a fool of yourself*).

The meaning here is a little different from the similar English proverb: "Haste makes waste." The English has to do with efficiency; the Russian has to do with personal worth.

Perhaps we can take to heart the moral of Поспешишь — людей насмешишь (and of "Haste makes waste") and proceed slowly with our task, учится по русски — going back to the beginning of this book and reading through, before starting our next chapter.

Chapter 9

Are You Learning Russian?

How much Russian language are you learning in this book?

You have seen how all the Russian letters look, in many different words. You have been learning hundreds of Russian words — many similar to English. You are getting the idea that Russian words change their endings to suit the time, the gender, the sentiment about and the size of objects, as well as to fit the position of the word in a sentence.

You have read many words in many kinds of sentences — sentences with information, with quotations, with questions and answers. You have read lines of dialogue and small stories, and verses, and several proverbs. Since folk and fairy tales are as familiar to Russian as to American children, perhaps you will like to read a few lines from Russian fairy tales. Look up the words which are new to you in the vocabulary at the back of the book.

American children know the following fairy tale as the story of Tom Thumb.

МАЛЬЧИК–С–ПАЛЬЧИК

Жил старик со старухою. Раз старуха рубила капусту и нечаянно отрубила палец. Завернула его в тряпку и положила на лавку.

Вдруг услышала — кто-то на лавке плачет. Развернула тряпку, а в ней лежит мальчик ростом с пальчик.

Удивилась старуха, испугалась:

— Ты кто таков?

— Я твой сынок, народился из твоего мизинчика.

Взяла его старуха, смотрит — мальчик крохотный-крохотный, еле от земли видно. И назвала его Мальчик-с-Пальчик.

The next folk fairy tale is the Russian version of "The Gingerbread Boy."

КОЛОБОК

Русская Народная Сказка

Жил-был старик со старухой. Вот и просит старик: "Испеки мне, старая, колобок." . . .

. . . Then that story follows on in a pattern of repetition about Kolobok's adventure in running away from everybody who is glad to meet him and wants to eat him. Here is part of the refrain in Kolobok's singsong:

> Я от дедушки ушёл,
> Я от бабушки ушёл,
> Я от зайца ушёл,
> Я от волка ушёл,
> От медведя ушёл,
> От тебя, лиса, не хитро уйти . . .

Since the same themes appear in folk and fairy tales of many countries, it is often difficult to establish in which country a particular story was created. However, the following excerpt does have a definite English origin — which can be heard in its Russian version.

ЖИЛ НА СВЕТЕ ЧЕЛОВЕК

Жил на свете человек —
Скрученные ножки,
И гулял он целый век
По скрученной дорожке.

Now turn from old folk literature to modern Russian writers, and read these brief excerpts in verse:

В. Маяковский

ЧТО ТАКОЕ ХОРОШО И ЧТО ТАКОЕ ПЛОХО

Крошка-сын
    к отцу пришёл,
и спросила кроха:
— "Что такое
    хорошо
и что такое
    плохо?" —

У меня
    секретов нет,
слушайте, детишки —
папы этого
    ответ
помещаю
    в книжке.

Two easy-to-translate verses:

Если мальчик
    любит труд,
тычет
    в книжку
        пальчик,
про такого
    пишут тут:
он
    хороший мальчик.

———

Этот
    чистит валенки,
моет
    сам
        калоши.
Он
    хотя и маленький,
но вполне хороший.

One of the most popular, if not *the* most popular, Soviet children's writer is S. Marshak, who writes in verse. Here is an excerpt from his famous *The Mail*.

С. Маршак

ПОЧТА

Кто стучится в дверь ко мне
С толстой сумкой на ремне,
С цифрой 5 на медной бляшке,
В синей форменной фуражке?
 Это он,
 Это он,
Ленинградский почтальон.

У него
Сегодня много
Писем
В сумке на боку —
Из Ташкента,
Таганрога,
Из Тамбова
И Баку.
В семь часов он начал дело,
В десять сумка похудела,
А к двенадцати часам
Всё разнёс по адресам.

. . . .

Нетрудно письму
Увидеть свет:
Ему
Не нужен билет,
На медные деньги
Объедет мир
Заклеенный
Пассажир.

Reading "Pochta" is an excellent review of the vocabulary in earlier chapters — it has names of cities, talk
of travel, use of numbers.

A great number of new books for Russian children, written in literary prose, have to do with nature, science and knowledge in general. One of the most famous popular-science writers is M. Ilin. Here is a sample from one of his many books:

М. Ильин

СТО ТЫСЯЧ ПОЧЕМУ

"Путешествие по Комнате"

. . . Люди знают, когда и кем изобретены телефон и электричество — а спросите их давно-ли придумано зеркало, носовой платок, давно-ли стали мыться мылом, есть картошку!

На эти вопросы очень немногие ответят.

Мы с удовольствием читаем о путешествиях по далёким странам и не догадываемся что в двух шагах от нас, а то и ближе, лежит незнакомая, удивительная, загадочная страна, которая называется: Наша Комната.

Did you notice the many everyday words, including *nose-kerchief* — "носовой платок," translated as *handkerchief* — in the section from Ilin?

The world-famous Russian writer L. N. Tolstoy, who died in the early part of the century, wrote many short stories for children which continue to be published, and read by Russian children, today. His stories deal with the nature of good and evil and the conscience of man. Here is one of his very short stories in its entirety:

Левь Николаевичʼ Толстой

НА ВОРЕ И ШАПКА ГОРИТ

Один мужик потерял деньги, и думал что кто-то их украл. Но он никак не мог найти вора. Сошлись мужики, и стали думать как узнать у кого деньги. Один мужик сказал: "А я знаю такое слово, что у вора шапка будет гореть." Один мужик взялся за шапку, и все узнали что он был вор."

In conclusion, the author wishes to say some confident Russian words directly to the reader.

Здравствуйте, дорогие американские читатели-ученики и дети!

Как интересно было познакомить вас немножко с русским языком!

Спасибо за ваше хорошее внимание.

Надеюсь что вы все теперь будете продолжать учиться по русски.

С уважением,
и до свидания!

— Маргарита Рудольф

———

КОНЕЦ (kah-ɴʏᴇʜᴛs) — THE END

Acknowledgments

The author extends grateful acknowledgment to Fenya Gurvich, until recently faculty member of the Kiev Pedagogical Institute, for critical attention to the grammatical accuracy, idiomatic wording, and clarity in the Russian portion of this book.

Also to an unpublished "Russian Grammar" by the late Morris Kellerman, which proved to be the most valuable reference work.

M. R.

Vocabulary

NOTE

Stress is indicated in the parentheses by CAPITAL LETTERS.

If a word is other than nominative singular, the regular nominative follows as part of the explanation.

Diminutives are followed by the usual form as part of the explanation.

A prepositional phrase for easier reference has the noun or pronoun first, in the Russian phrase; the English pronunciation gives the phrase as spoken. Thus: "вас, у (oo vahs). . ."

When not otherwise indicated, *a* is pronounced as in *comma*, *o* as in *obey*, *e* as in *met*, *i* as in *fit*, *u* as in *true*.

й is indicated by *y*, but it is almost one sound with a previous vowel: oy as in *boy;* ay as in *sky;* keey almost *key*, etc.

zh is as *s* in *pleasure*.

А а

a (ah) — and, while, but

август (AHV-goost) — August

автобусом (ahv-TO-boo-som) — (on a) bus; nom.: автобус (ahv-TO-boos)

автор (AHV-tor) — author

адресам, по (paw ah-dreh-SAHM) — to the addresses; nom. sing.: адрес (AH-drehs) — address

Азовское море (A-ZAWV-sko-yeh MAW-reh) — The Sea of Azov

акт (ahkt) — act

Александрович (Ah-lyehk-SAHN-dro-veech) — son of Alexander (Александр)

Александровна (Ah-lyehk-SAHN-drov-na) — daughter of Alexander

Алексеевич (Ah-lyehk-SEH-yeh-veech) — son of Aleksey (Алексей — Alexis)

Алексеевна (Ah-lyehk-SEH-yehv-na) — daughter of Aleksey

Алексей (Ahl-yehk-SEHY) — Alexis

Алёша (Ahl-YO-sha) — dim. of Алексей

Алёшка (Ahl-YO-shka) — further dim. of Алексей

Аляска (Ah-LYAH-ska) — Alaska

Америка (Ah-MEH-ree-ka) — America

125

американец (ah-meh-ree-кан-nyehts) — an American, masc. noun; американка (-nka), fem. noun

американская (ah-meh-ree-кahn-ska-yah) — American, fem. adj.; американский (-skeey), masc. adj.

американски, по (paw ah-meh-ree-кahn-skee)—in (the) American (way)

американские (ah-meh-ree-кahn-skee-yeh) — American, adj. pl.

Амур (Ah-moor) — Amur (River)

Андрей (Ahn-дреhy) — Andrew

английская (ahn-gleey-ska-yah) — English, fem. adj.; английский (-skeey), masc. adj.

английски, по (paw ahn-gleey-skee) — in English

английские (ahn-gleey-skee-yeh) — English, adj. plural

Аннечка (ahn-yeh-chka) — dim. of Анна (ahn-na) — Anna

Антон (Ahn-tawn) — Anthony

Анюта (Ah-nyoo-ta) — Anita, dim. of Анна

апрель (ah-prel) — April

АССР (Ah Ess Ess Err) — ASSR (Armenian Socialist Soviet Republic)

астронавт (ah-stro-наhvt) — astronaut; cosmonaut

астроном (ah-stro-nohm) — astronomer

атом (ah-tawm) — atom

африканец (ah-free-кан-nyehts) — an African, masc. noun

Африки (Ah-free-kee) — Africa

аэроплан (ah-eh-ro-plahn) — airplane

аэропорт (ah-eh-ro-port) — airport

Б б

Баба Яга (вah-ba Ya-gah) — Baba Yaga, a Russian fairy-tale witch

бабочка (вah-boch-ka) — butterfly

бабушка (вah-boosh-ka) — grandmother; pl.: бабушки (вah-boosh-kee) — grandmothers

бактерия (bahk-тyeh-ree-yah) — bacteria

Баку (Bah-koo) — Baku, a city

Балтимор (Bahl-tee-mawr) — Baltimore

баюшки баю (вah-yu-shkee bah-yu) — a Russian lullaby refrain

бедность (вehd-nost) — poverty

бежим (beh-zheem) — we run; we are running

без (behz) — without

белка (вyehl-ka) — squirrel; also, a dog's name

Белое море (вyeh-lo-yeh maw-reh) — the White Sea

библиотека (bee-blee-o-тeh-ka) — library

билет (bee-lyeht) — ticket

биография (bee-a-grah-fee-yah) — biography

биология (bee-a-lo-gee-yah) — biology

ближе (blee-zheh) — nearer

бляшке, на (na blyah-shkeh) — on a badge; nom.: бляшка (blyah-shka)

126

боку, на (na bah-кoo) — on a side; nom.: бок (bawk)

большой (bawl-shoy) — big, masc.

борщ (borshch) — borsch, a Russian soup

браво! (brah-vo) — bravo!

брат (braht) — brother

будет (boo-dyeht) — (he, she, it) will be, sing.; pl.: будут (boo-doot) — (they) will be

будете (boo-dyeh-tyeh) — (you) will be

буду (boo-doo) — I will

буква (book-va) — letter (of the alphabet); pl.: буквы (book-vi) — letters of the alphabet

булка (bool-ka) — white bread; roll

был (bil) — (he) was

была (bi-lah) — (she) was

было (bi-lo) — (it) was

В в

в (v) — in, at, to

важно (vazh-naw) — importantly

ваза (vah-za) — vase

валенки (vah-lyehn-kee) — Russian felt snow-boots

вам, к (k vahm) — to you

Ваня (vah-nyah) — Vanya, a boy's name, dim. of Иван (Ee-vahn)

Варвара (Vahr-vah-ra) — Barbara

вас, у (oo vahs) — with you; nom.: вас (vahs) — you

ваше (vah-she) — your, possessive neuter

Вашингтона (Vah-sheeng-ton-a) — from Washington; nom.: Вашингтон (Vah-sheeng-tawn)

вдруг (vdroog) — suddenly

вежливо (vehzh-lee-vo) — politely

вежливом, о (o vehzh-lee-vom) — (about) the polite . . ., masc. sing. adj.; nom.: вежливый (vehzh-lee-viy)

век (vehk) — century

Великий Океан (Vyeh-lee-keey O-keh-ahn) — the Pacific Ocean

великого (vyeh-lee-ko-vo) — of the great, adj., masc. sing. genitive; masc. sing. nom.: великий (vyeh-lee-keey)

верно (vyehr-no) — right, all right

весело (veh-syeh-lo) — gayety, fun

весна (vehs-nah) — spring

ветер (veh-tyehr) — wind

вечер (vyeh-chehr) — evening

взлетел (vzleh-tehl) — (he) flew up

взяла (vzyah-lah) — (she) took

взялся (vzyahl-sya) — (he) took a hold of

видит (vee-deet) — sees

видно (veed-no) — visible

визит (vee-zeet) — visit

вкусно (vkoos-no) — tasty

Владимир (Vlah-dee-meer) — Vladimir

Владимирович (Vlah-dee-mee-ro-veech) — son of Vladimir

внимание (vnee-mah-nee-yeh) — attention

внучек (vnoo-chek) — dim. of внук (vnook), grandson

внучка (VNOOCH-ka) — dim. of внука (VNOO-ka), granddaughter

во (vo) — in

водичка (vah-DEECH-ka) — dim. of вода (vah-DAH) — water

водка (VAWD-ka) — Russian liquor

воет (VO-yeht) — howls

возить (vaw-ZEET) — to pull, as to pull a sled

Волга (VOL-ga) — Volga (River)

влока (vol-KAH) — from the wolf; nom.: волк (volk)

вопрос (vah-PROS) — question

вопросы (va-PRO-si) — questions

вора (vo-RA) — thief; nom.: вор (vor)

воре, на (na VO-reh) — on the thief; nom.: вор (vor)

восемнадцать (vo-sehm-NAHD-tsat) — eighteen

восемь (VO-syehm) — eight

восемьдесят (vo-syehm-dyeh-SYAHT) — eighty

восемьсот (vo-syehm-SAWT) — eight hundred

восток (vah-STAWK) — east

вот (vawt) — here is, here's

вполне (vpahl-NYEH) — entirely

время (VREHM-yah) — time

всем (vsyehm) — to or for all, everybody; nom.: все (vsyeh)

всё (vsyaw) — all, everything

вставать (vstah-VAHT) — to get up

встанем (VSTAH-nyehm) — (we) will get up

встанет (VSTAH-nyeht) — (he, she, it) will get up

всякому (VSYAH-ko-moo) — (for)

every kind; nom.: всякий (VSYAH-keey)

въезде (VYEHZ-deh) — (about) arrival (by transportation); nom.: въезд (vyehzd)

вы (vi) — you, in the plural

выезд (VI-yehzd) — departure, exit (by transportation)

выйди (VIY-dee) — come out!

вытянул (VI-tya-nool) — (he) stretched

Г г

Гагарин, Юрий (YU-reey Gah-GAH-reen) — Yuri Gagarin

газеты (gah-ZYEH-ti) — newspapers; nom. sing.: газета (gah-ZYEH-ta)

где (gdyeh) — where?

географическая (geh-o-grah-FEE-cheh-ska-yah) geographical, fem. adj.

география (geh-o-GRAH-fee-yah) — geography

геология (geh-a-LO-gee-yah) — geology

героев (geh-RO-yehv) — (of the) heroes; nom. pl.: герои (geh-RO-ee)

глобус (GLAW-boos) — globe

говорит (ga-va-REET) — speaks, says

говорят (ga-va-RYAT) — they speak, they say

года (GAW-da) — (of the) year; nom.: год (gawd)

гора (gaw-RAH) — mountain

гореть (gaw-RYEHT) — to burn

горит (ga-REET) — burns

128

горло, во всё (vo vsyaw GOR-law) — with full throat, or, as loud as possible

город (GAW-rod) — city

города (gaw-ro-DAH) — cities

гости, в (v GOS-tee) — as a guest; nom.: гост (gost)

готов (gah-TOV) — ready, masc. sing.

готово (gah-TO-vo) — (it is) ready

грамматике (gram-MA-tee-kyeh) — grammar

Гриша (GREE-sha) — Grisha, dim. of Григорий (Gree-GAW-reey) — Gregory

гулял (goo-LYAHL) — (he) strolled

Д д

да (dah) — yes

давно (dahv-NOH) — long ago, once upon a time

давно-ли (dahv-NO-lee) — was it long ago?

дадут (dah-DOOT) — (they) will give

даёт (dah-YOT) — gives

даже (DAH-zheh) — even (as: "He can't even read")

дайте (DAHY-tyeh) — give (imperative)

дал (dahl) — (he) gave

дала (dah-LA) — (she) gave

далеко (dah-lyeh-KO) — far

далёким, по (paw dah-LYO-keem) — in the distant..., adj. pl.; nom.: далёкие (dah-LYO-kee-eh)

два, две, двое (dvah, dveh, DVO-yeh) — two: masc., fem., neut.

двадцать (DVAHD-tsat) — twenty

двенадцать (dveh-NAHD-tsat) — twelve

дверь (dvehr) — door

двести (DVYEH-stee) — two hundred

двух (dvookh) — two, genitive, of any gender; nom. masc.: два (dva); fem.: две (dveh); neuter: двое (DVO-yeh)

девочка (DYEH-vach-ka) — girl

девочки (DYEH-vach-kee) — girls

девяносто (dyehv-yah-NO-sto) — ninety

девятнадцать (dyehv-yaht-NAHD-tsat) — nineteen

девять (DYEHV-yaht) — nine

девятьсот (dyehv-yaht-SAWT) — nine hundred

деду (DYEH-doo) — for, or to, grandfather; nom. sing.: дед (dyehd)

дедушка (DYEH-doosh-ka) — grandfather, dim. of дед (dyehd), grandfather, old man; dim. pl.: дедушки (DYEH-doosh-kee)

декабрь (dyeh-KAHBR) — December

дело (DYEH-lo) — business, work

деньги (DYEHN-gee) — money, coins

Десна (Dyehs-NA) — Desna (River)

десять (DYEH-syaht) — ten

детей (dyeh-TYEHY) — children; nom.: дети (DYEH-tee); дитя (dee-TYAH), sing.

детишки (dyeh-TEESH-kee) — children (unusual dim. form)

дитя (dee-TYAH) — child

Днепр (Dnyehpr) — Dnieper (River)

до (daw) — until (*see* до свидания)

догадываемся (da-GAH-di-va-yehm-syah) — (we) are guessing

дожди (dahzh-DEE) — (to) rain, verb

дождик (DOZH-deek) — a little rain, dim. of дождь (dozhd) — rain

доктор (DOHK-tawr) — doctor

дома (DAW-ma) — (at) home, nom. sing.: дом (dawm) — house or home; pl.: дома (do-MAH)

домой (daw-MOY) — (toward) home, as in phrase "going home"; nom. sing.: дом (dawm)

дорогие (da-ra-GEE-yeh) — dears

дорожке, по (paw dah-RAWZH-keh) — on a little path; dim. of дорога (do-RO-ga)

до свидания (daw svee-DA-nee-ya) — good-by, or so long, till we meet again

другую (droo-GOO-yu) — other; nom.: другая (droo-GA-ya)

думает (DOO-ma-yeht) — thinks

думал (DOO-mahl) — (he) thought

думать (DOO-maht) — to think

дядя (DYAH-dyah) — uncle

Е е

Европа (Yeh-VRO-pa) — Europe

его (yeh-VO) — his, him, or it

его зовут (yeh-VO za-VOOT — he (is) called, or his name is, they call him)

Егорка (Yeh-GAWR-ka) — dim. of Егор (Yeh-GAWR) Igor

едет (YEH-dyeht) — goes, going, comes, coming (by transportation); pl.: едут (YEH-doot)

ей (YEHY) — to him

Екатерина (Yeh-kah-tyeh-REE-na) — Catherine

еле (YEH-lyeh) — hardly

ему (yeh-MOO) — (to) him; nom.: он (awn)

еры (yeh-RI) — name of the 29th letter of the Russian alphabet — ы

если (YEH-slee) — if

есть (yehst) — to eat; can also mean "is"

ещё (yeh-SHCHO) — still, or yet

Ё ё

ёлка (YOL-ka) — fir tree, or Christmas tree; pl.: ёлки (YOL-kee)

Ж ж

ждали (ZHDAH-lee) — (they) waited

ждут (zhdoot) — (they) wait

жена (zheh-NA) — wife (zh as *s* in *pleasure*)

Женя (ZHEH-nyah) — Zhenya, a boy's name

живут (zhee-VOOT) — (they) live

жил (zheel) — lived, or there lived, masc.

жил–был (zheel–bil — there once lived (used in folktales, as "once upon a time there lived"))

Житомир (Zhee-то-meer) — Zhitomir, a city

жить (zheet) — to live

жужжи (zhoozh-zнее) — buzz, verb

жужжит(zhoozh-zнеет) — buzzes

жук (zhook) — bug

Жуков (Zhoo-кawv) — Zhukov, last name, masc.

Жукова (Zhoo-ко-va) — Zhukova, last name, fem.

журнал (zhoor-naнl) — magazine; pl.: журналы (zhoor-nан-li)

З з

за (zah) — behind, beyond, onto, for

забора, у (oo zah-вон-ra) — by the fence; nom.: забор

завернула (zah-vehr-noo-la) — (she) wrapped

завтра (zaнv-tra) — tomorrow

завтрак (zaнv-trahk) — breakfast

загадочная (zah-gaн-dach-na-yah) — puzzling, fem. adj.

задал вопрос (zah-daнl vah-pros) — asked a question

зайца (zaй-tsa) — rabbit, genitive case; nom. sing.: заец (zaн-yehts)

заклеенный (zah-клҮеh-yehn-niy) — sealed, masc.

закричал (zah-kree-cнaнl) — (he) hollered

заметка (zah-меhт-ka) — note, or notice

замок (zah-мawк) — lock

запад (zaн-pahd) — west

здравствуй (zdraнst-vooy) — hello, sing. and familiar form

здравствуйте (zdraнst-vooy-tyeh) — hello, pl. and polite form

земли, с (s zyehm-lee) — from earth; nom.: земля (zyehm-lyaн)

зеркало (zҮehr-kah-lo) — mirror

зима (zee-маn) — winter

зимой (zee-moy) — during winter, or in winter

знаем (zna-yehm) — (we) know

знаете (zna-yeh-tyeh) — (you) know

знак (znahk) — sign

знаю (zna-yu) — (I) know

знают (zna-yut) — (they) know

зовут (za-voот) — (they) call

зоология (zaw-o-lo-gee-yah) — zoology

И и

и (ee) — and, also

Иван (Ee-vaнn) — Ivan, common Russian masc. name

Иванович (Ee-vaнn-no-veech) — son of Ivan

Ивановна (Ee-vaнn-nov-na) — daughter of Ivan

играл (ee-graнl) — (he) played

играть (ee-graнt) — to play

идёт (ee-dyoт) — goes

из (eez) — from

издалека (ee-zdahl-yeh-кa) — from afar

изобретены (ee-zob-reh-teh-NI) — invented

иностранец (ee-na-STRAH-nyets) — a foreigner, masc.

интересна (een-tyeh-REHS-na) — interesting, fem.

интересно (een-tyeh-REHS-no) — interesting, neuter

испеки (ee-speh-KEE) — bake

испугалась (ee-spoo-GAH-lahs) — (she became) frightened

их (eekh) — them

ищет (EE-shchyeht) — looks for, or, is looking for

ищут (EE-shchoot) — (they are) looking for

июль (ee-YUL) — July

июнь (ee-YUN) — June

Й й

йод (yohd) — iodine

К к

к (k) — to

Кавказ (Kahv-KAHZ) — the Caucasus

казак (kah-ZAHK) — cossack

как (kahk) — how, as

какао (kah-KAH-o) — cocoa

какая (kah-KAH-ya) — which, what (fem.)

какое (kah-ko-yeh) — which, what (neuter)

какому, по (paw kah-KOH-moo) — by which . . . ?

календарь (kahl-yehn-DAHR) — calendar

калоши (kah-LO-shee) — galoshes

Кама (KAH-ma) — Kama (River)

Канада (Kah-NAH-da) — Canada

Канаде, в (v kah-NAH-dyeh) — in Canada

капуста (kah-POO-sta) — cabbage; капусту (kah-POO-stoo) after certain verbs

Карское море (KAHR-sko-yeh MAW-reh) — Kara Sea

карта (KAHR-ta) — map

картошка (kahr-TOSH-ka) — potato, or, potatoes in general

касса (KAHS-sa) — ticket office, box office, cashier's booth

кататься (ka-TAT-syah) — riding

Катя (KAH-tyah) — dim. of Екатерина (Yeh-kah-tyeh-REE-na) — Catherine

качаю (kah-CHAH-yu) — (I) am rocking

каша (KAH-sha) — porridge

кем (kehm) — (by) whom

Киев (KEE-yehv) — Kiev, a city

кипит (kee-PEET) — is boiling, or boils

Клайборн, Вен (Vehn KLAHY-born) — Van Cliburn, the pianist

класс (klahss) — class

клетка (KLYEHT-ka) — cage

клеткой, с (s KLYEHT-koy) — with a cage

книга (KNEE-ga) — book; pl.: книги (KNEE-gee); accusative: книгу (KNEE-goo)

книжке, в (v KNEEZH-keh) — in the book; книжку (KNEEZH-koo) — book, genitive case; nom.: книжка (KNEEZH-ka) — another form for книга

ко (kaw) — to

когда (kag-DAH) — when

132

кого (ka-vo) — whom

коза (ka-zaн) — goat, fem.

колобок (ka-la-вок) — a little roll (in a folktale only)

Коля (Kol-yah) — Kolya, a boy's name

комета (kah-мен-ta) — comet

комната (кawm-na-ta) — room

комнате, в (v ком-nah-tyeh) — in the room

композитор (kam-pa-zee-tor) — composer

конец (kah-nyeнts) — (the) end

конфет (kahn-fyeнt) — candy, genitive case; nom.: конфеты (kahn-fyeн-ti)

концерт (kahn-tseнrt) — concert

корзинка (kar-zeeн-ka) — dim. of корзина (kar-zee-na) — basket

корзины (kar-zee-ni) — baskets

коробочка (ka-ro-bach-ka) — dim. of каробка (ka-rob-kah) — box

коса (ka-saн) — braid

космонавт (kos-mo-navt) — cosmonaut

космос (kos-mos) — cosmos, space

кот. *See* котик

котёнок (kah-tyaw-nawk) — kitten

котик (кaw-teek) — kitty, dim. of кот (kawt) — cat, masc., or of кошка (кawsh-ka) — cat, fem.

Котов (Kah-тawv) — Kotov, last name, masc.

Котова (Kah-taw-va) — Kotova, last name, fem.

которую (ka-tor-oo-yu) — genitive of которая (ka-то-ra-yah) — which, fem.

кофе (кaw-feh) — coffee

кошка. *See* котик

красивую (krah-see-voo-yu) — pretty, fem. genitive; nom.: красивая (krah-see-va-yah)

красивый (krah-see-viy) — handsome

красная (краhs-na-yah) — red, fem.

красное (краhs-no-yeh) — red, sing. neuter

кресло (кreнs-lo) — armchair

кроме (кro-meh) — besides

кроха (кro-kha) — little one, noun

крохотный (кro-khat-niy) — either: little, adj., or little one, masc. noun

крошка (кrosh-ka) — tiny little one; crumb

кто (ktaw) — who?

кто-то (ktaw–taw) — someone

куда (koo-da) — where

кукареку (koo-kah-reh-koo) — cock-a-doodle-doo!

куколка (koo-kal-ka) — dim. of кукла (кook-la) — doll

курорт (koo-rawrt) — resort

Курск (Koorsk) — Kursk, a city

кусок (koo-sawk) — a piece

кухня (кookн-nyah) — kitchen

кушать (koo-shaht) — to eat

Л л

лавке, на (na laнv-keh) or лавку (na laнv-koo) — on the bench; nom. sing.: лавка (laнv-ka) лампочка (LAHM-pach-ka) — dim. of лампа (LAHM-pa) — lamp

лежит (lyeh-ZHEET) — lies

Ленин (LYEH-neen) — Lenin, name of great Soviet leader

Ленинград (Lyeh-neen-GRAHD) — Leningrad, a city

ленинградской (lyeh-neen-GRAHD-skoy) — at or from Leningrad, adj.

лет (lyeht) — (of) years, genitive; *this* word is not used in nominative form

летом (LYEH-tawm) — during summer; nom. sing.: лето (LYEH-to)

Лиза (LEE-za) — Lisa

лиса (lee-SAH) — fox

литература (lee-tyeh-rah-TOO-ra) — literature

лицо (lee-TSO) — face

лодочка (LO-dach-ka) — dim. of лодка (LOD-ka) — rowboat

луне, на (na loo-NYEH) — on the moon; nom. sing.: луна (loo-NA) — moon

любит (LYOO-beet) — loves

любишь (LYOO-beesh) — (you, sing.) love

люблю (lyoo-BLYOO) — (I) love

людей (lyoo-DYEHY) — people; nom.: люди (LYOO-dee)

M м

май (my; rhymes with *sky*) — May, the month

мак (mahk) — poppy (flower or seed)

маленький (MAN-lyehn-keey) — little, or little one, masc.; as, " He is so little "; " He is such a little one."

малое (MAH-lo-yeh) — little (neuter)

мальчика (MAHL-chee-ka) genitive of boy, nom. sing.: мальчик (MAHL-cheek)

маме (MAH-meh) — for, or to mother

мамочка (MAH-mach-ka) — dim. of мама (MAH-ma) — mama

Марс (Mahrs) — Mars

марта, первого (PEHR-va-go MAHR-ta) — first of March; nom. sing.: март (mahrt) — March; Mar. 1 — первое марта (PEHR-vo-yeh MAHR-ta); in March — в марте (v MAHR-teh)

Маршак, Самуил (Mahr-SHAHK, Sa-MOOEEL) — Samuel Marshak, a writer

маршрут (mahrsh-ROOT) — route of travel

масло (MAHS-lo) — butter, oil

масса (MAHS-sa) — mass, " a lot of," bulk

матушка (MAH-too-shka)—mother

Машка (MAHSH-ka) — dim. of Маша (MAH-sha), Masha, girl's name (Maria)

мая (MAH-yah) — (of) May

Маяковский, Владимир (Ma-ya-KOHV-skeey, Vlah-DEE-meer) — Vladimir Mayakovsky, a poet

медведя (meh-DVEH-dya) — bear; nom.: медведь (mehd-VEHD)

медной, на (nah MEHD-noy) — on the copper, adj.

медные (МЕНD-ni-yeh) — copper, adj. pl.

меня, у (oo meh-NYAH) — I have

места, с (s МЕН-sta) — out of place; nom. sing.: место (МЕН-sto); pl.: места (meh-STAH)

мех (mehkh) — fur

меховая (МЕН-kha-va-yah) — fur, adj. fem.

мизинчика (mee-ZEEN-chee-ka) — the little finger; nom. sing.: мизинчик (mee-ZEEN-cheek)

милая (МЕЕ-la-yah) — darling, fem.

миллион (meel-lee-ON) — million

мило (МЕЕ-lo) — charming, cute

милый (МЕЕ-liy) — darling, masc.

Миннеаполис (Meen-neh-АН-po-lees) — Minneapolis

мир (meer) — peace, world

митинг (МЕЕ-teeng) — meeting

Миша (МЕЕ-sha) — Misha, a boy's name, dim. of Михаил (Mee-kha-EEL) — Michael

мне (mnyeh) — (to) me

много (MNAW-ga) — many, or much

мог (mohg) — (he) was able, or could

могу (ma-GOO) — (I) can

моет (МО-yeht) — washes, verb

моё (maw-YO) — my, neuter

моём (ma-YOM) — about my, masc. and neuter

можете (МОН-zheh-tyeh) — you can, or may

мои (mo-EE) — my, pl.

мой (moy) — mine or my, masc. (rhymes with *boy*)

молодец (maw-law-DETS) — a fine fellow

молоко (mah-lah-КО) — milk

море (МАW-reh) — sea

мороз (mah-ROZ) — frost

моря (МАWR-yah) — sea, genitive; nom. sing.: море (МАW-reh)

Москва (Mosk-VA) — Moscow, a city

Москву (Mosk-VOO) — to, or into, Moscow

мост (mawst) — bridge

мою (ma-YU) — my, fem.; nom.: моя (ma-YAH)

мудренее (moo-dreh-NYEH-yeh) — wiser

муж (moozh) — husband

мужик (moo-ZHEEK) — a peasant

мужики (moo-zhe-KEE) — peasants

Мурманск (Moor-MAHNSK) — Murmansk, a city

муха (MOO-kha) — a fly

мы (mi) — we (*i* as in *if*)

мыло (МIH-lo) — soap

мылом (МIH-lom) — (with) soap

мыться (МIT-syah) — to wash oneself

мягкий (МYAH-keey) — soft, masc.

Н н

на (nah) — on, to, for

надежда (nah-DYEHZH-da) — hope

надеюсь (nah-DYEH-yus) — (I) hope

назвала (nah-zVAH-la) — named

называется (nah-zi-VAH-yeh-tsyah) — (is) called

найти (nay-TEE) — to find

нам, к (k nahm) — to us, to our home; nom. sing.: мы (mi) — we

написан (nah-PEE-sahn) — is written, written by

напишу (nah-pee-SHOO) — (I) will write

народился (nah-ra-DEEL-syah) — born; a more usual word is родился (ro-DEEL-syah)

народная (nah-ROD-na-yah) — folk, fem. adj.

нас (nahs) — us

нас, у (oo nahs) — with us; nom. мы (mi) — we

насмешишь (nah-smeh-SHEESH) — (you) will make (people) laugh

Наташа (Nah-TAH-sha) — Natasha, girl's name

научиться (nah-oo-CHEET-syah) — to learn, or to succeed in learning

наций (NAH-tseey) — (of) nations, genitive; nom.: нации (NAH-tsee-ee)

начал (nah-CHAHL) — (he) began

наш (nahsh) — our, masc.

наша (NAH-sha) — our, fem.

наши (NAH-shee) — our, pl.

нашей (NAH-shehy) — our, sing.

нашёл (nah-SHYOL) — (he) found

нашла (nahsh-LA) — (she) found

нашли (nahsh-LEE) — (they) found

нашу (NAH-shoo) — our, fem. sing.

не (nyeh) — not

Нева (NYEH-va) — Neva (River)

него, у (oo neh-VO) — ("to him") — he has

незнакомая (nyehz-nah-KO-ma-yah) — strange, fem. adj.

ней, к (k nyehy) — to her

немногие (nyeh-MNAW-gee-yeh) — few

немного (nyeh-MNAW-go) — not much, not many, or a few, a little

немножко (nyeh-MNOH-zhko) — a little

нет (nyeht) — no

нетрудно (nyeh-TROOD-no) — without difficulty

нету (NYEH-too) — there isn't

нечаянно (nyeh-CHA-yahn-no) — accidentally

ни (nee) — neither, or nor

никак (nee-KAHK) — in no way

Никита (Nee-KEE-ta) — Nikita, man's name

Николай (Nee-kaw-LAY) — Nicholas

Ниночка (NEE-nach-ka) — Ninochka, dim. of Нина (NEE-na) — Nina

ничего (nee-cheh-VO) — nothing

нищий (NEE-shcheey) — poor, or pauper

но (no) — but

новому. *See* новую

новую (NO-voo-yu) — new, fem. genitive; nom.: новоя (NO-vo-yah); к Новому Году (k NO-vo-moo GAW-doo) — for the New Year

ножки (NOHZH-kee) — little legs, or little feet

носовой (na-sa-VOY) — pertaining to the nose, masc. adj.

ноябрь (no-YAHBR) — November

нужен (NOO-zhehn) — needed, necessary, masc.

нужна (NOO-zhna) — needed, necessary, fem.

няня (NYAH-nyah) — nursemaid

О о

о (aw) — about

О (Oh) — Oh!

обе (O-byeh) — both, fem.

обед (ah-BEHD) — dinner

обещали (a-byeh-SHCHAH-lee) — promised, pl.

обратно (aw-BRAHT-no) — on a return trip

объедет (a-BYEH-dyeht) — will ride (completely) around, encircle

объединённые (ob-yeh-dee-NYON-nyeh) — united, adj. pl.; genitive: объединённых (ob-yeh-dee-NYON-nikh)

овощами, с (s O-va-shcha-mee) — with vegetables

овощи (O-va-shchee) — vegetables

Одесса (O-DYEHS-sa) — Odessa, a city

один (a-DEEN) — one, masc. Also одна, -дно (a-DNA, -DNO) nom. sing., fem. and neuter; одну (a-DNOO) — fem. genitive

одиннадцать (a-DEE-nahd-tsat) — eleven

озеро (O-zyeh-ro) — lake

означает (oh-zna-CHA-yet) — designate, or stand for

Ока (Oh-KAH) — Oka (River)

океан (a-keh-AHN) — ocean

окно (awk-NO) — window

около (O-kaw-lo) — near

октябрь (ok-TYAHBR) — October

он (awn) — he

она (a-NAH) — she

они (a-NEE) — they

оно (aw-NO) — it

О О Н (Oh Oh Enn) — Organization of United Nations (UN)

опасно (aw-PAH-sno) — dangerous

организация (or-gah-nee-ZAH-tsee-yah) — organization

ос (aws) — wasps; nom. sing.: оса (aw-SAH)

остался (as-TAHL-sya) — he remained

остаток (ahs-TAH-tok) — remainder, leftover

остров (OH-strov) — island; pl. острова (o-stro-VA)

от (awt) — from

ответ (at-VYEHT) — answer, noun

ответили (at-VYEH-tee-lee) — (they) answered

ответят (at-VYEH-tyaht) — (they) will answer

откуда (at-KOO-da) — from where

отрубила (a-troo-BEE-la) — (she) chopped off

оттуда (at-TOO-da) — from there

отцу (aht-TSOO) — (to) father; nom.: отец (ah-TETS)

Ox! (Okh!) — Oh!

очень (O-chehn) — very

П п

пальчик (PAHL-cheek) — dim. of палец (PAH-lehts) — finger

папочка (PAH-pach-ka) — dim. of папа (PAH-pa) — dad, father, papa папы (PAH-pi) — father's

парад (pah-RAHD) — parade

Париж (Pah-REEZH) — Paris

пассажир (pahs-sah-ZHEER) — passenger

пахнет (PAHKH-nyeht) — smells

первого (PEHR-va-go) — first; nom.: первый

переводе, в (v peh-reh-VO-deh) — in translation

песенку (PEH-syehn-koo)—a song; dim.: песенка (PEH-syen-ka); accusative: песню (PEHS-nyoo)

Петрович (Pyeh-TRO-veech) — son of Peter

Петровна (Peh-TRO-vna) — daughter of Peter

петух (peh-TOOKH) — rooster

Пётр (Pyotr) — Peter; dim.: Петя (PEH-tyah)

пианист (pee-ah-NEEST) — pianist

писать (pee-SAHT) — to write

писем (PEE-sehm) — of letters; nom.: письма (PEE-sma)

письму (pee-SMOO) — for a letter

пишу (pee-SHOO) — (I) write

пишут (PEE-shoot) — (they) write

пища (PEE-shcha) — food

планета (plah-NYEH-ta) — planet

плачет (PLAH-cheht) — (he) is crying

плоток (pla-TAWK) — kerchief

плохо (PLO-kho) — bad

по (paw) — on, or along, also before name of language; as, *I read Russian: "Я читаю по русски"*

поговорить (pa-ga-va-REET) — to talk some, converse

погода (pa-GO-da) — weather

подарков (pa-DAHR-kov) — of presents, genitive; nom. sing.: подарки (pa-DAHR-kee)

подбежал[а] (pad-be-ZHAHL[a]) — he [she] ran up to

подожди (pa-dazh-DEE) — wait!

поедем (PO-eh-dyem) — (we) are going

поедет (pa-YEH-dyeht) — (he) will ride, or will go

поедут (paw-YEH-doot) — will go (by transportation)

поездка (pa-YEHZD-ka) — a trip

поем (pa-YEHM) — (I) will eat

поёт (pa-YOT) — sings

поживаете (pa-zhee-VA-yeh-tyeh) — getting along

пожнёшь (pazh-NYAWSH) — (you) will reap

познакомить (po-znah-KO-meet) — to acquaint

пойдём (pay-DYOM) — let's go

пойду (pay-DOO) — I will go

покормит (pa-KOR-meet) — (he or she) will feed

покушаем (pa-koo-sha-yehm) — (we) will eat

покушали (pa-koo-shah-lee) — (they) ate

пол (pawl) — floor; pl.: полы (paw-LI)

полный (POL-nihy) — full, masc.

положила (pa-la-zhee-la) — (she) laid down

Полтава (Pol-TAH-va) — Poltava, a city

помещаю (pa-meh-SHCHA-yu) — (I) place

помогут (pa-ma-GOOT) — (they) will help

понимать (pa-nee-MAHT) — to understand

понимаю (pa-nee-MA-yu) — (I) understand

понюхай (pah-NYOO-khay)—smell

попили (paw-pee-LEE) — they took a drink, finished drinking; попить (pa-PEET) — to take a drink

популярна (pa-poo-LYAHR-na) — popular, fem.

популярная (pa-poo-LYAHR-na-yah) — popular, fem. (slightly different from above)

пора (pa-RAH) — (it's) time

порок (pa-ROK) — sin, or vice

посеешь (pa-SYEH-yehsh) — (you) will sow

после (PAW-slyeh) — after

послезавтра (paw-slyeh-ZAHV-tra) — day after tomorrow

посмотрел (pa-sma-TREHL) — (he) took a look, or a look around

поспешишь (pa-speh-SHEESH) — (you) will hurry

потерял (pa-tyeh-RYAHL) — (he) lost

потом (pa-TOME) — afterward, or then

потому (pa-ta-MOO) — because

похудела (pa-khoo-DYEH-la) — (she) grew thin

почему (pa-cheh-MOO) — why

почта (PAWCH-ta) — mail

почтальон (pawch-tah-LYON) — postman

поэма (pa-EH-ma) — poem

поэт (pa-EHT) — poet

поэтому (pa-EH-ta-moo) — for this reason, or therefore

пою (pa-YU) — (I) sing

правда (PRAHV-da) — truth; also name of newspaper

праздник (PRAHZ-dneek) — holiday

прекрасная (preh-KRAHS-na-ya) — very beautiful, or splendid, fem.

прекрасно (preh-KRAHS-no) — splendid

прибежали (pree-beh-ZHAH-lee) — (they) came running

прибежим (pree-beh-ZHEEM) — (we) will come running

пригласите (pree-gla-SEE-tyeh) — (you) invite

придумала (pree-DOO-mah-la) — (she) thought up, or made up

придумано (pree-DOO-ma-no) — (were) invented, discovered, or first thought of

приедет (pree-YEH-dyet) — will arrive

прийдут (preey-DOOT) — (they) will come

прийти (PREEY-tee) — to come

прилетел (pree-lyeh-TYEHL) — (he) flew in

принесёт (pree-neh-SYAWT) — (he or she) will bring

принёс (pree-NYAWS) — (he) brought

принц (preents) — prince

пришёл (pree-SHYOL) — (he) came

пришли (preesh-LEE) — (they) came

приятно (pree-YAHT-no) — pleasant

про (proh) — about

продолжать (praw-dol-ZHYAT) — to continue

просит (PRO-seet) — (he) begs, or pleads; вот просит — and so he begs прочитаю (pro-chee-TA-yu) — (I) will read through

путешествие (poo-tyeh-SHEST-vee-yeh) — travel

путешествиях, о (о poo-tyeh-SHEST-vee-yahkh) — about travels

пятнадцать (pyaht-NAHD-tsat) fifteen

пять (pyaht) — five

пятьдесят (pyaht-dyeh-SYAHT) — fifty

пятьсот (pyaht-SAWT) — five hundred

Р р

работает (rah-BO-ta-yeht)—works

работать (rah-BOH-taht) — to work

радостно (RAH-dast-no) — happy, glad

раз (rahz) — once

развернула (rahz-vehr-NOO-la) — (she) unwrapped

разговор (rahz-ga-VOR) — conversation

разнёс (rahz-NYOS) — (he) distributed by carrying

ракета (rah-KEH-ta) — rocket

рано (RAH-no) — early

рано утром (RAH-no OO-trom) — early in (the) morning

рассказ (rahs-SKAHZ) — story

река (reh-KA) — river

ремне, на (na rem-NYEH) — on a (leather) strap

республик (rehs-POOB-leek) — republics, gen.; nom. sing.: республика (rehs-POOB-lee-ka)

ресторан (res-to-RAHN) — restaurant

Ростов (Ros-TAWv) — Rostov, a city

ростом (ROS-tom) — the size of (referring to growing things)

рубила (roo-BEE-la) — (she) chopped

русская (ROOS-ska-ya) — Russian, fem. adj.

русски, по (paw ROOS-skee) — in Russian (language)

русский (ROOS-skeey) — Russian, masc. noun and adj.

русским (ROOS-skeem) — Russian, adj.

русских (ROOS-skeekh) — Russian, adj. pl., genitive; nom. adj. pl.: русские (ROOS-skee-yeh)

русского (ROOS-ska-vo) — of the Russian . . . , adj., masc., genitive

русском, на (na ROOS-skom) — in Russian

русском переводе, в (v ROOS-kom peh-reh-VO-dyeh) — in Russian translation

рыба (RI-ba) — fish; pl.: рыбы (RI-bi)

рыбака (ri-bah-KA) — fisherman, genitive case; nom. sing.: рыбак (ri-BAHK)

рыбаке, о (aw ri-bah-KEH) — about a fisherman

рыбаки (ri-bah-KEE) — fishermen

рыбке, о (o RIB-keh) — about a little fish

рыболов (ri-ba-LOV) — fisherman

рыболову (ri-ba-LO-voo) — (to) the fisherman

С с

с (s) — from, out of, with

салат (sah-LAHT) — salad, lettuce

сам (sahm) — himself (pronoun); (by) himself

сама (sah-MA) — herself (pronoun); (by) herself

самоварчик (sah-mo-VAHR-cheek) — dim. of самовар (sah-mo-VAHR), samovar, a Russian urn for boiling water

самого, у (oo SA-mo-go) — by the very edge

самое (SAH-mo-yeh) — the most, neuter adv.; самое главное (SAH-mo-yeh GLAHV-no-yeh) — the most important (thing), or the main thing

саночки (SAH-noch-kee) — a child's sled

Саратов (Sah-RAH-tov) — Saratov, a city

Саша (SAH-sha) — Sasha, boy's name

Сашка (SAHSH-ka) — dim. of Sasha

сварила (svah-REE-la) — (she) cooked

свежий (SVEH-zheey) — fresh, masc.

свет (sveht) — light, world

свете, на (na SVEH-tyeh) — in the world

светлая (SVEHT-la-ya) — light, adj. fem.

свидания. See до свидания

своего (svo-yeh-VO) — his, her or its

своё (sva-YO) — its, or its own

свою (sva-YU) — her

сдвинул (SDVEE-nool) — (he) moved

Севан (Syeh-VAHN) — Sevan, a lake

север (SYEH-vehr) — north

Северное море (SYEH-vehr-no-yeh MAW-reh) — the North Sea

сегодня (syeh-VOD-nyah) — today

седеть (syeh-DYENT) — to grow gray

секретов (syeh-KREH-tov) — secrets, genitive; nom.: секреты (syeh-KREH-ti)

село (syeh-LO) — village

семнадцать (syehm-NAHD-tsat) — seventeen

семь (syehm) — seven

семьдесят (syehm-dyeh-SYAT) — seventy

семьсот (syehm-SAWT) — seven hundred

сентябрь (syehn-TYAHBR) — September

Серёжа (Seh-RYO-zha) — boy's name, dim. of Сергей (Sehr-GEHY) — Sergei

сестричка (syeh-STREECH-ka) — dim. of сестра (syeh-STRAH) — sister

сём, о (aw syohm) — about this

Сибирь (See-BEER) — Siberia

сидел (see-DYEHL) — (he) sat, (he) has been sitting

синей, в (v SEE-nyehy) — in a blue

синий (SEE-neey) — blue, masc.

сказал (skah-ZAHL) — (he) said

сказала (skah-ZAH-la) — (she) said

сказали (SKAH-zah-lee) — (they) said

сказано (SKAH-zah-no) — (it) is said

сказка (SKAHZ-ka) — fairy tale

скоро (SKAW-ro) — soon

скрученные (SKROO-chehn-ni-yeh) — crooked, masc. adj.; скрученной (SKROO-chehn-no-yeh) — crooked, neuter adj. (agreeing with noun after prep.)

слива (SLEE-va) — plum

сливы (SLEE-vi) — plums

слов (slawv) — of words; nom. pl.: слова (slo-VAH)

слово (SLAW-vo) — word, nom.

слушайте (SLOO-sha-y-tyeh) — listen

слушали (SLOO-shah-lee) — (they) listened

слышно (SLIHSH-na) — it is heard, audible

смешно (smesh-NO) — funny

смотрел (sma-TREHL) — (he) looked

смотрела (sma-TREH-la) — (she) looked

смотреть (sma-TRYENT) — to look

смотрит (SMO-treet) — (he or she) looks

снега (SNYEH-ga) — (of) snow; nom. sing.: снег (snyehg)

Снегурочка (Snyeh-GOO-rach-ka) — the Snow Maiden (a fairy-tale character)

со (so) — with (same as с)

собаке, о (aw sa-BAH-keh)—about a dog; nom. sing.: собака (sa-BAH-ka) — dog, fem.; plural: собаки (sa-BAH-kee)

советских (sa-VYEHT-skeekh) — Soviet, adj. pl., genitive; nom.: советские (sa-VYEHT-skee-yeh)

советское (sa-VYEHT-sko-yeh) — Soviet, neuter adj.

советы (sa-VYEH-ti) — advice

совсем (sahv-SYEHM) — entirely, at all (as in "nothing at all," "not at all")

соединённые (so-yeh-dee-NYON-ni-eh) — united, pl.

сок (sawk) — juice

солнышко (SOL-nish-ko) — sun, dim. of солнце (SOL-ntseh)

сорок (SO-rawk) — forty

социалистических (so-tsee-ah-lee-STEE-cheh-skeekh) — social-ist, adj. pl. genitive; nom.: социалистические (so-tsee-ah-lee-STEE-cheh-skee-yeh)

Сочи (SOH-chee) — Sochi, a city

сошлись (sa-SHLEES) — (they) came together

союз (SA-yuz) — union

спасибо (spah-SEE-bo) — thank you

спать (spaht) — to sleep

спросила (spra-SEE-la) — (she) asked

спросите (spra-SEE-tyeh) — ask!

спутники (SPOOT-nee-kee) — trav-eling companions, satellites; nom. sing.: спутник (SPOOT-neek)

среду, в (v SREH-doo) — on Wed-nesday; nom. sing.: среда (sreh-DAH) — Wednesday

С С С Р (Ess Ess Ess Err) — U S S R

стакан (stah-KAHN) — glass (for drinking)

стали (STAH-lee) — (they) began, became

станцию (STAHN-tsee-yu) — sta-

tion; nom. sing.: станция
(STAHN-tsee-yah)

старая (STA-rah-ya) — old one,
old, noun or adj., fem.

старик (STA-reek) — old man

старухой, со, or старухою, со (so
stah-ROO-khoy, so stah-ROO-kho-
yu)—with the old woman; nom.
sing.: старуха (stah-ROO-kha)

стена (styeh-NAH) — wall

сто (sto) — hundred

стол (stawl) — table

столы (staw-LI) — tables

сторонам, по (paw sto-ro-NAHM)
— from side to side

стране, в (v strah-NYEH) — in the
country; nom. sing.: страна
(strah-NA); pl. genitive: странам (strah-NAHM); nom.:
страны (STRAH-nih)

стрелка (STRYEHL-ka) — Little
Arrow; name of a dog

стуле, на (na STOO-lyeh) — on the
chair; nom.: стулы (STOOL-i)

стучится (stoo-CHEE-tsyah) — is
knocking

суббота (soob-BO-ta) — Saturday;
в субботу (v soob-BO-too) — on
Saturday

судят (SOO-dyaht) — (they)
judge

сумка (SOOM-ka) — bag

сумке, в (v SOOM-keh) — in the
bag; с сумкой (s SOOM-koy) —
with a bag; nom. sing.:
сумка (SOOM-ka)

суп (soop) — soup

С Ш А (Ess Shah Ah) — U S A

съеду (s-YEH-doo) — (I) will take
a ride to, or I'll go to

съем (s-YEHM) — I'll eat up

сынок (sih-NAWK) — dim. of сын
(sihn) — son

сыночек (sih-NO-chek) — further
dim. of сын (sihn) — son

Сэндбург, Карл (Kahrl SEND-
boorg) — Carl Sandburg

Т т

табаком, с (s tah-bah-KOM) —
with tobacco; nom. sing.: табак (tah-BAHK)

Таганрога, с (s Ta-gan-RO-ga) —
from Taganrog, a city

так (tahk) — so, thus

такого (tah-KAW-vo) — such, this
kind, genitive case; nom. sing.
masc.: таков (tah-KOHV); neuter: такое (ta-KAW-yeh), такой
(ta-KOY)

таком, о (aw ta-KAWM) — about
such

там (tahm) — there

Тамбова, из (eez Tam-BAW-va) —
from Tambov, a city

Ташкента, из (eez Tahsh-KEN-ta)
— from Tashkent, a city

твёрдый (TVYOR-diy) — hard,
masc.

твоего (tva-yeh-VO) — yours, familiar, nom.: твой (tvoy)

твоё (tva-YO) — your, familiar
form, neuter

театр (TEH-ah-tr) — theater

тебя (tyehb-YAH) — you, familiar,
genitive; nom. sing.: ты (ti)

телефон (tyeh-lyeh-FON) — tele-
phone

тема (TYEH-ma) — theme

темнеет (tyehm-NYEH-yeht) — it
is getting dark

143

темно (tyehm-NO) — dark

теперь (tyeh-PEHR) — now

тепло (tyeh-PLO) — warm

тесно (TYEH-sno) — crowded

тесто (TYEH-sta) — of dough, genitive; nom. sing.: тесто (TYEH-sto)

тётя (TYO-tyah) — aunty

тихо (TEE-kha) — quiet

тише (TEE-sheh) — quieter

то (taw) — that, neuter

товарищ (to-VAH-reeshch) — comrade

товарищи (to-VAH-ree-shchee) — comrades

тогда (tahg-DAH) — then

тоже (TO-zheh) — also

ток (tawk) — current

Толстой, Левь Николаевич (Lyehv Nee-ka-LAH-yeh-veech Tal-STAWY) — Leo Nikolayevich Tolstoy

толстой, с (s TAWL-stoy) — with a thick, adj.

том, о (aw tome) — about that

тост (tawst) — toast (as in offering a toast)

тот (tawt) — that, masc.

три (tree) — three, masc. and fem.

тридцать (TREED-tsat) — thirty

тринадцать (tree-NAHD-tsat) — thirteen

триста (TREE-sta) — three hundred

трое (TRO-yeh) — three, neuter

тройка (TROY-ka) — team of three horses

трубочка (TROO-bach-ka) — dim. of трубка (TROOB-ka) — pipe

труд (trood) — labor

трудно (TROOD-na) — difficult

тряпку, в (v TRYAHP-koo) — in a rag; nom. sing.: тряпка (TRYAHP-ka)

туда (too-DAH) — there

тут (toot) — here

ты (ti) — you, the familiar form

тысяча (TI-syah-cha) — thousand

тычет (TI-cheht) — pokes

У у

у (oo) — by

уважением, с (s oo-vah-ZHEN-nee-yehm) — respectfully

увидеть (oo-VEE-dyeht) — to see

удалец (oo-da-LETS) — a brave one

удивилась (oo-dee-VEE-lahs) — (she) was surprised

удивительная (oo-dee-vee-TEHL-na-yah) — wonderful

удовольствием, с (s oo-da-VOLST-vee-yehm) — with pleasure

уедет (oo-YEH-deht) — goes away

уже (oo-ZHEN) — already

ужин (OO-zheen) — supper

узнали (oo-ZNAH-lee) — (they) recognized

узнать (oo-ZNAHT) — to recognize

уйти (ooy-TEE) — to go away

украинец (oo-krah-EE-nyehts) — Ukrainian, noun, masc.

украински, по (paw oo-krah-EEN-skee) — in Ukrainian (language)

украинские (oo-krah-EEN-skee-yeh) — Ukrainian, adj. pl.

украл (oo-KRAHL) — (he) stole

улице, на (na OO-lee-tseh) — on the street; nom., улица (OO-lee-tsa) — street

144

улыбка (oo-LIHB-ka) — smile

умыто (oo-MIH-to) — washed

Урал (Oo-RAHL) — Urals, a mountainous region

услышала (oo-SLI-shah-la) — (she) heard

УССР (Oo Ess Ess Err) (USSR — Ukrainian Soviet Socialist Republic

утро (OO-tro) — morning

утром (OO-tram) — in the morning

утром, рано (RAH-no OO-tram) — early in the morning

ухо (OO-kho) — ear

уходи (oo-kha-DEE) — go away! (command)

учениками (oo-cheh-nee-KAH-mee) — with students

ученики (oo-cheh-nee-KEE) — students, pupils; sing.: ученик (oo-cheh-NEEK)

учитесь (OO-chee-tyehs) — (you) are learning

учится (oo-CHEET-syah) — to learn

учить (oo-CHEET) — to teach

ушёл (oo-SHYOL) — (I, masc.) went away, got away from

ушла, ушёл, ушли (oosh-LA, oosh-YOL, oosh-LEE) — she, he, they went

Ф ф

февраль (fev-RAHL) — February

физиология (fee-zee-a-LO-gee-yah) — physiology

флаг (flahg) — flag

форменной, в (v FOR-mehn-noy) — in a uniform, adj.

фотографии (fo-to-GRAH-fee-ee) — photographs

фотография (fo-to-GRAH-fee-yah) — photograph, photography

фруктами, с (s FROOK-tahm-ee) with fruits; фруктов (FROOK-tav) — of fruits, gen. pl.; nom.: фрукты (FROOK-ti) — fruits

фуражка (foo-RAHZH-ka) — cap

фуражке (foo-RAHZH-keh) — cap, after preposition

X x

ха-ха-ха (kha–kha–kha) — ha-ha-ha (laughter)

хижина (KHEE-zhee-na) — cabin

хитро (KHEE-tra) — complicated (or clever)

хлеб (khlyehb) — bread

холодно (KHO-lad-no) — cold

хорошая (kha-RO-sha-ya) — good, fem. adj.

хорошие (kha-RO-shee-yeh) — good, adj. pl.

хороший (kha-RO-sheey) — good, masc. adj.

хорошо (kha-ra-SHO) — good, fine

хорошое (kha-RO-sho-yeh) — good, neuter adj.

хотя (kha-TYAH) — although

хохот (KHO-khot) — laughter

хочу (kha-CHOO) — (I) want

Ц ц

цвет (tsvyeht) — color, also flower

целый (TSEH-liy) — whole, masc.

цена (tsyeh-NAH) — price

центр (tsehntr) — center

цирк (tseerk) — circus

цифра (TSEE-fra) — number, cipher

цифрой, с (s TSEE-froy) — with a number

цыплёнок (tsee-PLYO-nawk) — little chick

Ч ч

чай (chay) — tea

Чайковский, Пётр Ильич (Pyotr Eel-y-EECH Chay-конv-skeey) — Peter Ilyich Tchaikovsky, the composer

чайник (CHAY-neek) — teapot

чайничек (CHAY-nee-chek) — dim. of teapot

часам, к . . . (k . . . chah-SAHM) — toward . . . o'clock. *See* часов

часов (chah-SOHV) — hours; nom.: часы (chah-SI) — clock, watch, or hours

часто (CHAH-sto) — often

человек (cheh-lo-VEHK) — a person, a man

через (CHEH-ryehz) — across

Чернигов, в (v Chehr-NEE-gov) — to Chernigov (a city)

Чернигова, из (eez Chehr-NEE-gov-a) — from Chernigov

четверг (cheht-VEHRG) — Thursday

четыре (cheh-TI-reh) — four

четыреста (cheh-TI-reh-sta) — four hundred

четырнадцать (cheh-TIR-nahd-tsat) — fourteen

чёрного (CHOHR-naw-vo) — black; nom.: чёрный (CHOHR-niy)

Чёрное море (CHOHR-no-yeh MAW-reh) — (the) Black Sea

чижике (CHEE-zhee-keh) — (about a) siskin; nom.: чижик (CHEE-zheek) — a common European finch

Чили (CHEE-lee) — Chile

чистит (CHEES-teet) — cleans

читаем (chee-TAH-yehm) — (we) read, or reading

читали (chee-TAH-lee) — read, past tense, pl.

читатели (chee-TAH-tyeh-lee) — readers

читать (chee-TAHT) — to read

читаю (chee-TAH-yu) — (I) read, or am reading

читают (chee-TAH-yoot) — (they) read

что (shto) — what, or (conj.) that

что такое (shto tah-KO-yeh) — what (is) . . .?

что-то (SHTO-to) — something

Ш ш

шагах (sha-GAKH) — steps; nom.: шаги (sha-GEE)

шапочка (SHAH-pach-ka) — dim. of шапка (SHAHP-ka) — hat

шестнадцать (shehst-NAHD-tsat) — sixteen

шесть (shehst) — six

шестьдесят (shehst-dyeh-SYAT) — sixty

шестьсот (shehst-SAWT) — six hundred

шею (SHEH-yoo) — neck; nom.: шея

школа (SHKAW-la) — school

штат (shtaht) — state; pl.: штаты (SHTA-ti)

шум (shoom) — noise

шутки (SHOOT-kee) — jokes; nom. sing.: шутка

Ш-ш (sh-sh) — shush, or hush

Щ щ

щека (shcheh-KAH) — cheek

Э э

эволюция (eh-va-LYOO-tsee-ya) — evolution

экватор (eh-KVAH-tawr) — equator

экзамен (ehk-ZAH-mehn) — examination, or exam

экономист (eh-ko-naw-MEEST) — economist

экскурсия (ehks-KOOR-see-yah) — excursion

эксперимент (ehks-peh-ree-MEHNT) — experiment

электричество (eh-lehk-TREE-chest-vo) — electricity

энергия (eh-NEHR-gee-yah) — energy

Эрик (EH-reek) — Erik, boy's

эта (EH-ta) — this, fem.

эти (EH-tee) — these

это (EH-to) — this, neuter

этого (EH-ta-vo) — this one; nom.: этот (EH-tawt)

эхо (EH-kho) — echo

Ю ю

юному (YU-na-moo) — young

Юрий (YU-reey) — Yuri, man's name

Я я

я (yah) — I

ягод (YAH-gad) — berries (when you say "Let's pick berries"); nom. plural: ягоды (YAH-ga-di); nom. singular: яагода (YAH-ga-da) — a berry

языком (yah-zi-KOM) — (in a) language, or tongue; nom. sing.: язык

я ли не (yah lee neh) — am I not?

Ялта (YAHL-ta) — Yalta, a city

январь (Yahn-VAHR) — January